"This generation of Christians inhabit cu[...] only biblical revelation about reality, but a[...] Questions for Restless Minds series poses [...] of the toughest questions faced by young Christians to some of the world's foremost Christian thinkers and leaders. Along the way, this series seeks to help the Christian next generation to learn how to think biblically when they face questions in years to come that perhaps no one yet sees coming."

—Russell Moore,

public theologian, *Christianity Today*

"If you're hungry to go deeper in your faith, wrestle with hard questions, and are dissatisfied with the shallow content on your social media newsfeed, you'll really appreciate this series of thoughtful deep dives on critically important topics like faith, the Bible, friendship, sexuality, philosophy, and more. As you engage with some world-class Christian scholars, you'll be encouraged, equipped, challenged, and above all invited to love God more with your heart, soul, mind, and strength."

—Andy Kim,

multiethnic resource director, InterVarsity Christian Fellowship

"Rob Smith is the ideal person to tackle this particular question for restless minds. I know of few people who have approached this issue with such careful attention both to what the Bible says that might bear on this issue and how Christ's people might care for those who are struggling or distressed by it. This is an issue where emotions are running high at the moment, misinformation abounds, and, tragically, great harm is being caused. Rob is aware of the pain and the need for a gentle word. He is also aware of the goodness of God's word, the need to study it carefully, and so to speak a true word. I very gladly commend this book."

—Mark D. Thompson,

principal, Moore Theological College

"The 'Transgender Revolution' in society has a two-fold impact. An increasing number of people are suffering: the victims of a damaging ideology, who may not necessarily seek to promote it themselves. On the other hand, there are the campaigners and activists who aggressively promote gender ideology. Robert Smith presents a biblical and thoughtful response to their claims. With that firm foundation in place, he then offers wise and compassionate pastoral advice to address the needs of those who have been impacted by this cultural revolution."

—Sharon James,

social policy analyst, The Christian Institute, UK;
author of *Gender Ideology: What Do Christians Need to Know?*

How Should We Think about Gender and Identity?

Questions for Restless Minds

Questions for Restless Minds

How Should We Think about Gender and Identity?

Robert S. Smith

D. A. Carson,
Series Editor

LEXHAM PRESS

How Should We Think about Gender and Identity?
Questions for Restless Minds, edited by D. A. Carson

Copyright 2022 Christ on Campus Initiative

Lexham Press, 1313 Commercial St., Bellingham, WA 98225
LexhamPress.com

Print ISBN 9781683595151
Digital ISBN 9781683595168
Library of Congress Control Number 2021937705

Lexham Editorial: Todd Hains, Abigail Stocker, Kelsey Matthews, Mandi Newell
Cover Design: Brittany Schrock
Interior Design and Typesetting: Abigail Stocker

The Christ on Campus Initiative exists to inspire students on college and university campuses to think wisely, act with conviction, and become more Christlike by providing relevant and excellent evangelical resources on contemporary issues.

Visit christoncampuscci.org.

Contents

Series Preface

D. A. CARSON, SERIES EDITOR

T HE ORIGIN OF this series of books lies with a group of faculty from Trinity Evangelical Divinity School (TEDS), under the leadership of Scott Manetsch. We wanted to address topics faced by today's undergraduates, especially those from Christian homes and churches.

If you are one such student, you already know what we have in mind. You know that most churches, however encouraging they may be, are not equipped to prepare you for what you will face when you enroll at university.

It's not as if you've never known any winsome atheists before going to college; it's not as if you've never thought about Islam, or the credibility of the New Testament documents, or the nature of friendship, or gender identity, or how the claims of Jesus sound too exclusive and rather narrow, or the nature of evil. But up until now you've probably thought about such things within the shielding cocoon of a community of faith.

Now you are at college, and the communities in which you are embedded often find Christian perspectives to be at best oddly quaint and old-fashioned, if not repulsive. To use the current jargon, it's easy to become socialized into a new community, a new world.

How shall you respond? You could, of course, withdraw a little: just buckle down and study computer science or Roman history (or whatever your subject is) and refuse to engage with others. Or you could throw over your Christian heritage as something that belongs to your immature years and buy into the cultural package that surrounds you. Or—and this is what we hope you will do—you could become better informed.

But how shall you go about this? On any disputed topic, you do not have the time, and probably not the interest, to bury yourself in a couple of dozen volumes written by experts for experts. And if you did, that would be on *one* topic—and there are scores of topics that will grab the attention of the inquisitive student. On the other hand, brief pamphlets with predictable answers couched in safe slogans will prove to be neither attractive nor convincing.

So we have adopted a middle course. We have written short books pitched at undergraduates who want arguments that are accessible and stimulating, but invariably courteous. The material is comprehensive enough that it has become an important resource for pastors and other campus leaders who devote their energies to work with students. Each book ends with a brief annotated bibliography and study questions, intended for readers who want to probe a little further.

Lexham Press is making this series available as attractive print books and in digital formats (ebook and Logos resource). We hope and pray you will find them helpful and convincing.

1

INTRODUCTION

O N JANUARY 1, 2021, the newly re-elected Speaker of the United States House of Representatives, Nancy Pelosi, and Rules Committee Chairman, James P. McGovern, introduced a new set of house rules for the 117th Congress "and for other purposes."[1] According to the new rules, which are purported to promote diversity and inclusivity, words like "father," "mother," "son," "daughter," "brother" and "sister" are no longer to be used. The gender-neutral terms "parent," "child" and "sibling" are now to take their place. Similarly, "himself" and "herself" are to be replaced by "themself."

Meanwhile, across the pond in the south of England, maternity staff at Brighton and Sussex University Hospitals NHS Trust have been advised to stop using the terms "breastfeeding" and "breastmilk," and instead to speak of "chestfeeding" and "human milk."[2] A new policy issued by the Trust aims "to be inclusive of trans and non-binary birthing people without excluding the language of women or motherhood."[3] For female parents, then, "mothers and birthing parents" are the acceptable options, and a male parent can either be referred to as a "father or second biological parent."

Closer to home (for me), Dr. Holly Lawford-Smith, a political philosopher at the University of Melbourne, has recently found herself under personal and professional attack for raising concerns about legislative changes that are allowing transwomen (i.e., biological males who identify as women) open access to women-only spaces (e.g., changing rooms, fitting rooms, bathrooms, shelters, rape and domestic violence refuges, gyms, spas, schools, and prisons) and women-only activities (e.g., female sports, shortlists, prizes, quotas, clubs, events, festivals, and dating apps).[4]

These are far from isolated developments. They are simply three recent examples of numerous similar developments taking place across the Western world. But each is an instance of, and a sign of the steady advance of, what many have for some time been calling "The Transgender Revolution."[5]

The progress of this revolution not only tends to provoke polarized reactions, but inevitably raises important questions—questions about what is *real* and questions about what is *moral*. The reality question boils down to this: Is it really the case that someone can be born with "the wrong body," or is the person who feels this way simply confused about their identity or unhappy with their body? The morality question follows on from this, but has numerous faces to it, as well as various social, relational, and legal implications. For example, should children with gender identity concerns be given puberty blockers? Should a person be allowed to use the bathroom that corresponds to their subjective gender identity? Should Medicaid pay for sex reassignment surgery? Should a transwoman be allowed to compete in women's sports?[6] How should we regard the marriage of a woman to a transman or vice versa?

Understandably, differing answers to these questions tend to polarize people. But it's important to realize that behind the surface polarization lie two very different understandings of what gender is and how it is determined. The older understanding (sometimes called biological essentialism) claims that a person's gender is determined by the objective fact of their biological sex. Where there is a felt mismatch, then subjectivity should be helped to yield to objectivity. The newer understanding (sometimes called psychological essentialism) claims that the objective facts of biology do not determine a person's gender. This is determined by their gender identity—their own subjective sense of who and what they are.

In light of such a divide, and the social, medical, political, and legislative changes being wrought by the widespread acceptance of transgender claims, Christians have an urgent need to search the Scriptures carefully and prayerfully to see how God would have us think about and respond to such revolutionary developments. The main purpose of this short book is to begin such a search and to outline such a response.

2

KEY TERMS
AND THEIR
MEANINGS

$\mathbf{B}$ EFORE WE PROCEED, it will help us to clarify a number of key terms that are a basic part of the current discussion.

Biological sex, birth sex, or natal sex: These terms all refer to the physical or physiological characteristics that help us differentiate between males and females: chromosomes, hormones, gonads, genitals, and secondary sex characteristics—for example, body shape, voice pitch, and hair distribution. Biological sex is often simply referred to as "sex."[7]

Gender: Historically, the terms sex and gender have often been used interchangeably. Even today drawing a distinction between them is not universal. Where a distinction is made, gender is "often intended to emphasize the social and cultural, as opposed to the biological, distinctions between the sexes."[8] Increasingly, the psychological dimension of gender is included in the term. Gender, then, usually encompasses three aspects: gender identity, gender expression and gender roles.

Gender identity: This refers to the way individuals perceive themselves and conceive of themselves. When a person's subjective gender identity aligns with their objective sex, which is the case for most people, they are sometimes

referred to as being *cisgender* (cis = on the *same* side of).[9]
When there is a clash, however, then they are commonly
referred to as *transgender* (trans = on the *other* side of).
See further below.

Gender expression: This refers to the social or cultural
aspects of how masculinity and femininity are presented in
things like dress and demeanor, tastes and interests, social
conventions, and other gender norms. These vary from
culture to culture, if not from person to person.

Gender roles: This refers to the commonly accepted expectations of maleness or femaleness, including social and
behavioral expectations. While some roles (for example,
who cooks the meals or mows the lawn) vary from household to household or culture to culture, and often change
over time, others are biologically determined (most obvi-
ously, pregnancy and breastfeeding).

Gender bending: This refers to the intentional crossing or
bending or blending of accepted gender norms in a given
culture. This is done either by adopting the dress, man-
nerisms, roles, or behaviors of the opposite gender (e.g.,
transvestitism or gender nonconformity), or through the
attempt to obscure one's gender and to appear as either
asexual, agender, pansexual, omnigender, androgynous, or
non-binary.

Gender dysphoria: This is the latest diagnostic term for the distress experienced by those whose psychological gender identity differs from their biological sex (*DSM*-V, 2013).[10] It replaces the term *Gender Identity Disorder*, which saw the mismatch itself as a psychiatric disorder (*DSM*-IV, 1994). Now, however, it's only the distress that is (normally) caused by gender incongruence that is regarded as a problem, not the incongruence itself.[11] For this reason, I will use the term gender dysphoria only occasionally in this book and, for the most part, prefer the language of gender incongruence, which I deem to be a more helpful descriptor of the condition.

Intersex: This is a term that covers a range of disorders of sex development (DSDs) where there is some biological ambiguity in a person's genitalia or gonads, or more rarely still, their chromosomes. Except in very rare instances, a person's biological sex can be known from their DNA. Because intersex conditions are medically identifiable deviations from the binary sexual norm they are not regarded as constituting a third sex.[12] Because they are biologically (rather than psychologically) based, some intersex people do not wish to be associated with the LGBTQ+ movement.[13]

Transgender (or, increasingly, *trans*): This is an umbrella term for people who are born either male or female, but whose gender identity differs from their birth sex (in some degree), and who want to express the gender with which they identify through some form of social transitioning (e.g., changing their name and/or cross-dressing), if not cross-sex hormone therapy (CHT), if not also sex reassignment surgery (SRS).[14] Because of its breadth, the trans umbrella also includes those who identify as bigender, pangender, ambigender, omnigender, gender fluid, gender diverse, non-binary, or agender.

Cisheteronormativity: This is the view that biological sex is either male or female (gender binarism), that sex and gender are meant to match up (cisnormativitiy), and that only sexual orientation toward and sexual relations with a member of the opposite sex is natural (heteronormativity). As we will see, the ideas conveyed by the term cisheteronormativity are central to the biblical view of sex and gender. However, because these ideas are increasingly regarded as bigoted, oppressive, homophobic, and transphobic (especially by LGBTQ+ activists and allies), cisheteronormativity is a somewhat tainted term.

With these terms and definitions understood, we now turn to look more closely at contemporary gender theory and the revolutionary changes it is introducing to our culture.

3

THE
BRAVE NEW
WORLDVIEW
OF GENDER
PLASTICITY

"**W**HO AM I?" is by no means a new question. It is part of King David's query: "what is man that you are mindful of him, and the son of man that you care for him?" (Ps 8:4). Nevertheless, as the rapid development of new terminology testifies, it is being asked today with a new force and in a new form. The old form assumes there is an objective "I" that already exists and is simply waiting to be discovered. But this, according to current gender theory, is a false assumption. So the new form of the question is this: "*What do I identify as?*" This way of putting things emphasizes chosenness (as opposed to *giveness*) and possible change-ability (as opposed to *stability*).[15]

This takes us directly into the heart of the "brave new worldview" of gender plasticity. The word plasticity is important, for at the heart of this worldview lie the twin notions of "gender diversity" and "gender fluidity." Gender diversity conveys the idea that gender is not binary (either male or female) but exists on a broad spectrum with many points lying in between (or outside) male and female. One list on Tumblr, for example, currently lists close to 400 different gender options.[16] Gender fluidity conveys the idea that people can move back and forth along the gender spectrum. This idea is so acceptable to many millennials

(Gen Y) and post-millennials (Gen Z)—that is, those born after 1984—that they have been dubbed "the gender-fluid generation."[17]

It is also important to understand how these two notions—gender diversity and gender fluidity—are connected. For even if biological sex is understood to be binary (male and female)—which is still the generally accepted view (notwithstanding the acknowledgement of intersex deviations), once gender is severed from sex, then not only does gender not have to correspond to sex, but there is no reason for gender to share the binary character of sex. Here's how one biologically female advocate, who describes herself as "gender fluid but also non-binary and trans," puts it:

> My gender is an evolving thing, like my sexuality, the more I explore it the more it changes. The only reason why I feel I should put a label on it is just to make it easier for other people.[18]

However, not all who place themselves under the "T" umbrella are quite so ready to embrace the prospect of perpetual fluidity, nor to dispense with the sex/gender binary. In fact, many who identify as transgender have a very strong sense of the gender binary, at least in regard to their own experience. For example, those who experience gender incongruence are often convinced they are in "the wrong body" and therefore want their body to be (or be changed to appear to be) that of the opposite sex. In other words, they don't believe in gender diversity, nor are they interested in gender fluidity or gender neutrality. This is one of many tensions within the LGBTQ+ movement.

Nevertheless, the slender but common thread that seeks to hold the "T," "Q," and "A" letters in the ever-expanding acronym together is the idea that subjective feelings of identity necessarily override objective facts of biology. This is what has given rise to the "Self-ID" view of trans—i.e., if you say you're trans, then you are trans. The ideas at work here are (1) that gender identity is innate; (2) that self-identification is infallible; and (3) that self-declaration is, therefore, unchallengeable. Hence the familiar slogans—"transwomen are women" / "transmen are men"—and the legislative changes that have followed in their wake. For example, since January 2019, those who identify as transgender and non-binary in California have been able to change their gender on their state ID cards and driver's licences without having to go through a medicalized application process. In other words, no diagnosis of gender dysphoria is needed in order for a man to be legally recognized as a woman.[19]

Such developments beg the questions: Where did this revolution come from? And how has it come upon us so suddenly?

THE TRANSGENDER "TIPPING POINT"

Social commentators are generally agreed that sometime toward the end of 2013, Western society reached a transgender tipping point[20]—triggered in part by the success of the TV series *Orange is the New Black*.[21] Sociologically speaking, a tipping point refers to that moment in time when a minority is able to change the attitude of the majority—a change that presupposes the weakening, if not the collapse, of long-held understandings and assumptions.

But despite the appearance of suddenness, the larger change didn't, in fact, take place overnight. It has been happening incrementally for the last century or more.[22] Indeed, it is simply one part of a much broader moral, social, and sexual revolution that has engulfed Western culture—a revolution that includes the advent of the contraceptive pill, the various waves of feminism, pre-marital sexual experimentation, de facto marriage, no-fault divorce, abortion on demand, the lowering of film and television standards, the explosion of the pornography industry, the decriminalization of homosexual acts, and the legalization of same-sex adoption and same-sex marriage.

What's more, ever since the late 1960s, the transgender revolution—both politically and ideologically—has been intertwined with both the feminist and gay rights revolutions. Yet because it has been tucked in behind them (sometimes quite deliberately so, due to the gay lobby's uneasiness with their transgender compatriots) most Westerners hadn't felt its force, recognized its significance, or seen its implications. For at the heart of the transgender revolution, as we've already noted, is a new way of thinking about gender.

Central to this new way of thinking is the idea that gender itself (and not simply gender roles or gender expression) is entirely a social construct and not in any way biologically determined. The seeds of this idea came out of feminism (e.g., Simone de Beauvoir's famous statement: "One is not born, but becomes a woman"),[23] but were then refracted through gay and lesbian studies into queer ideology or gender theory. How so? The logical line of development is as follows: If being born a female and becoming a woman are two different things (so feminist ideology), and if there is no necessary correlation between your biological sex and your sexual orientation (so gay and lesbian thought), then why should there be any necessary correlation between your biological sex and your gender identity (so queer theory)?[24]

In other words, this new way of thinking not only draws a sharp distinction between sex and gender, but severs the connection. Sex is still generally seen as an objective biological reality, but it is not determinative of gender.

What then determines gender? Answers vary. For some, gender is determined by one's own choice (gender voluntarism); for others, by social and relational forces (gender constructivism); for yet others, by independent neurological factors[25] (gender determinism); and for others still, by some combination of factors. For most trans theorists, however, the answer is simple: gender is determined by gender identity—the social by the psychological.

Whatever the case, there is no necessary connection between any person's biological sex and their gender identity. The fact that they do align for most people is purely accidental (or perhaps a result of social conditioning). But there's no reason why they should align for any us. Consequently, more and more people are choosing to identify not only as transgender, but (as we've already noted) as pangender, bigender, trigender, multigender, omnigender, agender, gender fluid, gender diverse, gender queer, nonbinary, etc. Hence it is increasingly common to find an asterisk after the word trans, stylizing it as trans*, to indicated that it is being used "as a broad umbrella term to include a whole range of identities that aren't strictly *transgender.*"[26]

QUEER THEORY AND THE END OF GENDER

If this were not revolutionary enough, some want to take things even further. For example, the ultimate goal of some queer theorists is freedom from gender itself! In other words, they not only want to eliminate heteronormativity and banish binary categories, but jettison completely the very concept of gender. As one advocate has put it: "At the heart of Queer culture is revolution. The truest rebellion against a world built on categories, labels and binaries is coming from the emergence of identities that refuse to conform."[27] Queer theorist, Judith Butler, states it this way:

> The prospect of being anything, even for pay, has always produced in me a certain anxiety, "to be" gay,

"to be" lesbian seems to be more than a simple injunction to become who or what I already am ... I am not at ease with lesbian theories, gay theories, for identity categories tend to be instruments of regulatory regimes.[28]

Butler, therefore, posits that gender is not something a person *has* but something a person *does*; it is reiterated rather than received, performed rather than possessed. For this reason, any notion of gender norms necessarily "operates as a preemptive and violent circumscription of reality."[29] In fact, she even puts forward the idea that sex "is as culturally constructed as gender; indeed, perhaps it was always already gender, with the consequence that the distinction between sex and gender turns out to be no distinction at all."[30]

Only slightly less extreme ideas are being propounded by queer theologians. The late Virginia Ramey Mollenkott, for example, suggested that:

All of us are therefore called to confront the binary gender construct for our own good and the good of those who are transgender. Because gender roles are by no means equitable, binary gender assumptions and roles are devastating to all of us—"masculine" men, "feminine" women, and those somewhere in the middle.[31]

Mollenkott, therefore, anticipates and champions an omnigender future in which everyone "would have their own unique sexuality, falling in love with another person because of their emotional response to the person's entire being, not the person's genitals."[32] In such a future, birth certificates and driver licences would not record a person's sex or gender, individuals would be free to change their bodies by any means available, and all bathrooms, sports, and even prisons would be unisex. Those who fear such a prospect, Mollenkott claims, are reacting "out of loyalty to the idea that there really is an essential feminine and masculine binary that is either God's will or nature's perpetual norm or both."[33]

THE SHAPE OF THE FUTURE

This is the future that trans activists are seeking to realize and, in large measure, have already achieved. Not surprisingly, it's one that is proving testing for many Christians—particularly those who voice their opposition to gender ideology.

This is certainly what Dr. David Mackereth, an English disability assessor from Dudley, West Midlands, discovered in 2019. Mackereth lost his job after revealing to a supervisor that although he would have no issue using whatever first name service users wished him to use, he would not be able to address transgender clients by their chosen pronouns. "As a Christian," he said, "I would not be able to accede to such a request in good conscience."[34] Although he appealed his dismissal, an employment tribunal dismissed his appeal, stating that "belief in Genesis 1:27, lack of belief in transgenderism and conscientious objection to trans-genderism in our judgment are incompatible with human dignity and conflict with the fundamental rights of others, specifically here, transgender individuals."[35]

Amazon's recent erasure of Ryan Anderson's 2018 book, *When Harry Became Sally*, from its cyber shelves is another example. Despite selling the book for the last three years, Amazon justified this step on the grounds that it "reserves the right to pull any book ... that it believes violate company content guidelines on hate speech and other issues."[36] Yet it has not revealed at what point or in what way Anderson's book falls foul of these guidelines. Moreover, the fact that it is still selling Adolf Hitler's *Mein Kampf* suggests that the issue is not hate speech but the challenge the book poses to a current form of cultural orthodoxy.[37]

Finally, and once again closer to (my) home, the Australian state of Victoria has recently passed the "Change or Suppression (Conversion) Practices Prohibition Bill 2020 (Vic),"[38] which will make it unlawful for anyone (parent, pastor, teacher, counselor, friend) to provide assistance or encouragement to any person of any age to obey the Bible's teaching on sex and gender, even those "who explicitly and with full understanding request such help."[39] According to an explanatory memorandum, the bill's intention is to "denounce and prohibit" a "broad range of conduct, including, informal practices, ... that encourage change or suppression of sexual orientation or gender identity."[40] In other words, any Christian who falls short of affirming a trans person's gender identity risks falling foul of the bill!

These examples could be multiplied many times over. Each is a clear indicator of where many Western societies are either fast heading or have already arrived. This should not surprise us, however. The transgender revolution has been brewing for at least half a century. This is why, in a 2016 op-ed piece, *New York Times* columnist Frank Bruni could write that there is "a clear movement in our society toward L.G.B.T. equality, a trajectory with only one shape and only one direction."[41] This was confident, triumphant language, to be sure, but it was not without a basis then, and it has even more of a basis now.

HOW SHOULD CHRISTIANS RESPOND?

I raise these matters not to promote fear—far less, outrage—but to highlight the fact that Christians cannot hide from the transgender revolution. The transgender tipping point is well and truly behind us, and the revolution is unfolding all around us. While we are also seeing some signs of societal resistance, if not push back,[42] as long as the revolution is with us, it is imperative that we work out how God would have us respond to it.

The first and fundamental responsibility of every Christian is to live by every word that comes from the mouth of God, irrespective of whether our culture makes this easy or hard. This means we need to listen carefully to what the Bible teaches us about human sexuality and gender identity and then tease out how we live, love, and minister in a deeply confused and increasingly hostile culture, and to the many confused individuals within it (if not within our churches also).

This, in turn, means that we have both a pastoral task and a political task. Both are important, although some of God's people will be better able to engage in one more than the other. As we now turn to examine the Scriptures, my primary interest is in the pastoral implications of the Bible's teaching—that is, how to help precious people in our church, rather than how to combat a pernicious ideology in our culture.[43] So let me flag up front the key pastoral questions we need to answer so that we might be alert to how the Bible's teaching speaks to them and helps us think about them:

- How do we teach and encourage those who are conflicted and confused by the social changes going on around us?

- How do we counsel and care for those who, through no obvious fault of their own, experience a profound sense of gender incongruence?

- How do we effectively evangelize gender non-conforming people?

- What does repentance mean for someone who has transitioned gender?

- What does Christian discipleship look like for someone who battles ongoing gender dysphoria?

4

BIBLICAL AND
THEOLOGICAL
EXPLORATION

I T'S TAKEN US a little while to get here, but we now come to the most important of our tasks: engaging with the word of God in Scripture. Under the following headings, my aim is to explore some of the chief ways in which the Bible's teaching speaks to the issues raised by the transgender revolution and the phenomenon of gender incongruence. In terms of method, I will be combining a biblical theological approach (which seeks to be sensitive to the unfolding nature of the Bible's teaching) with a systematic theological approach (which is concerned to synthesize the Bible's overall teaching), while keeping an eye on the pastoral questions raised above and addressing them at appropriate points along the way.

THE BINARY NATURE OF SEX

With refreshing clarity, the basic, binary and dimorphic nature of human sex is revealed in the creation account of Genesis 1 and then repeated in Genesis 5:

> Then God said, "Let us make man in our image." …
> So God created man in his own image,
>   in the image of God he created him;
>   male [*zakhar*] and female [*neqevah*]
>   he created them. (Gen 1:26–27)

33

When God created man, he made him in the like-
ness of God. Male and female he created them, and
he blessed them and named them Man when they
were created. (Gen 5:1b–2)

The implication of these texts is plain: God has created
no third sex! This was not only the case before humanity's
fall into sin (hereafter "the fall"), as we see in Genesis 1, but
it remains the case after the fall, as we see in Genesis 5. Lest
we be in any doubt, this point is underlined by none other
than Jesus himself. In answering a question about divorce
posed by the Pharisees, he references Genesis 1:27 (and
1:1 also), interpolating the word "from" to indicate that the
binary nature of human sex is not only an ongoing fact but
one with ongoing implications:

Have you not read that he who created them from the
beginning made them male and female. (Matt 19:4;
compare Mark 10:6)

While we will say a little more about the reality of intersex conditions shortly, it is important to realise that all
such DSDs, like every other kind of disorder, disease, or
disability, are postlapsarian (i.e., "after the fall") phenom-
ena, not part of the "very good" creation "in the beginning"
(Gen 1:1, 31).[44] Moreover, far from contradicting the teaching of either Genesis or Jesus, such conditions are normally,
and rightly, classified as "medically identifiable deviations
from the human binary sexual norm."[45] In other words,

male and female are not two extremes at either end of a broad continuum, and, as we've already noted, the intersexed are not a third sex. From the beginning of creation, God made human beings male and female and either male or female, despite the difficulty we may have (on extremely rare occasions) of determining a person's sex.[46]

THE RELATIONSHIP BETWEEN SEX AND GENDER

The binary nature of human sex revealed in Genesis 1 is both emphasised and developed in Genesis 2. Here we move from humanity being described in terms of the adjectives male (*zakhar*) and female (*neqevah*)—which are not unique to humans but also apply to animals (e.g., Gen 6:19)—to the nouns man (*'ish*) and woman (*'ishshah*), as these are applied to Adam and Eve:

> Therefore a man [*'ish*] shall leave his father and his mother and hold fast to his wife [*'ishshah*], and they shall become one flesh. And the man and his wife were both naked and were not ashamed. (Gen 2:24–25)[47]

The clear implication of this move from male and female (in Gen 1) to man and woman (in Gen 2), an implication everywhere confirmed as the biblical narrative unfolds, is that a person's biological sex reveals and determines both their objective gender (what gender they, in fact, are) and certain key gender roles (should they be taken up). That is, human males grow into men (and potentially husbands and fathers) and human females grow into women (and potentially wives and mothers).[48] Indeed, it is this set of binary connections that makes human marriage possible. As Jesus again confirms—bringing Genesis 1 and 2 into the closest possible connection:

> But from the beginning of creation, "God made them male and female." "Therefore a man shall leave his father and mother and hold fast to his wife, and the two shall become one flesh." (Mark 10:6–8a)

Furthermore, in fulfillment of God's purpose that humanity should "be fruitful and multiply and fill the earth" (Gen 1:28), it is out of the "one flesh" union of male and female (as husband and wife) that children are (normally) conceived and brought into the world—children who perpetuate not only the sex and gender binary but the sex and gender connection. The Hebrew language of the Old Testament expresses this dual reality at every stage of personal development and in every station of life. For example:

- son (*ben*) and daughter (*bat*)
- boy (*yeled*) and girl (*yalda*)
- brother (*'ach*) and sister (*'achot*)
- young man (*na'ar*) and young woman (*na'arah*)

- bridegroom (*chatan*) and bride (*kalla*)

- father (*'av*) and mother (*'em*)

- father-in-law (*cham*) and mother-in-law (*chamot*)

- uncle (*dod*) and aunt (*dodah*)

- manservant (*'eved*) and maidservant (*'amah*)

- prophet (*navi'*) and prophetess (*nevi'ah*)

- prince (*sar*) and princess (*sarah*)

- king (*melek*) and queen (*malka*)

In summary: a person's biological sex reveals their actual gender, determines their true gender identity, and establishes certain potential gender roles.[49] For example, only a male can truly be a son and truly become a father. Only a female can truly be a daughter and truly become a mother.[50] Furthermore, man and woman are not two poles at either end of a gender spectrum. Indeed, as we've already seen (and will see further shortly), there is simply no space in biblical anthropology—either before or after the fall—for additional sexes and/or additional genders.

THE IMPACT OF THE FALL

This is not to say that the Bible presents human sex and gender after the fall, outside the garden of Eden, as straight-forward. To the contrary, it plainly teaches that the entrance of sin has had a catastrophic effect on every part of our humanity. Not only have our hearts and minds become corrupt, but our bodies, like the rest of the created order, have been "subjected to frustration" and are "in bondage to decay" (Rom 8:20–21; compare v. 23 NIV). In other words, because sin and death have permeated both ourselves and our world, all kinds of things go wrong with us—both psychologically (with our minds) and physiologically (with our bodies).

One of the many ways the Bible acknowledges this latter fact is by introducing us to the category of the eunuch.[51] In fact, in Matthew 19, following his discussion of the nature of marriage and the possible grounds for divorce and remarriage, Jesus distinguishes between three types of eunuchs: two literal and one metaphorical.

> For there are eunuchs who have been so from birth, and there are eunuchs who have been made eunuchs by men, and there are eunuchs who have made themselves eunuchs for the sake of the kingdom of heaven. Let the one who is able to receive this receive it. (Matt 19:12)

Leaving aside Jesus' third category (which refers to those who have denied themselves marriage in order to serve God's kingdom),[52] his first two categories were, almost certainly, informed by the common Jewish distinction between "eunuchs of the sun"—that is, those who have been eunuchs from the moment they first saw the sun (i.e., from birth)—and "eunuchs of man"—that is, man-made eunuchs, either by accident or deliberately. The first of these categories would, most likely, have encompassed a number of the conditions that today are included under the "intersex" umbrella.[53]

Whatever might be said of the status of eunuchs in later Christian reflection,[54] it is important to repeat the point made earlier: Scripture does not present eunuchs as either a third sex or a third gender.[55] In fact, every eunuch we meet in Scripture is presented as male (as is indicated by the use of masculine verbs and male pronouns). Eunuchs are simply males who are unable to function sexually or procreatively (Isa 56:3)—either because of a birth defect or due to human intervention. Otherwise put, Scripture resists diluting the sex/gender binary, even though some do not fit neatly into it.

DUALISTIC HOLISM OR HOLISTIC DUALITY

But what about those whose biological sex is unproblematic, but who claim to have been born in the wrong body? For example, how do we make sense of a biological male who sincerely believes he is a woman? Can a female soul end up in a male body or vice versa? Is this a genuine possibility outside the Garden of Eden? To answer this question, we need to consider the Bible's teaching on the relationship between the physical (or corporeal) and nonphysical (or incorporeal) aspects of human beings.

The biblical authors display a variety of different ways of speaking about these two anthropological aspects.[56] What is consistently taught in both Testaments, however, is a dichotomous or bipartite view.[57] That is, human beings consist of two distinct elements: body and soul.[58] Furthermore, while the body perishes at death, and so can be separated from the soul, God's intention is for it to be reunited with the soul in resurrection at the last judgment. This, for example, is what enables Jesus to speak in the following way:

> And do not be afraid of those who kill the body but cannot kill the soul. Rather be afraid of the One who can destroy both soul and body in hell. (Matt 10:28 NIV)

At the same time, the biblical authors view the human person as an integrated whole. As John Cooper writes: "Biological processes are not just functions of the body as distinct from the soul or spirit, and mental and spiritual capacities are not seated exclusively in the soul or spirit. All capacities and functions belong to the human being as a whole, a fleshly-spiritual totality."[59] In other words, Scripture understands "human beings holistically as single entities which are psychosomatic unities."[60] We are dealing, then, with a both-and: an ontological duality (a distinct body and soul) within a functional holism (an integrated person).

Otherwise put, and without wanting to minimize the reality of the psychological distress experienced by sufferers of gender incongruence, there is simply no space within biblical anthropology for the kind of ontological mismatch that is sometimes claimed. *The soul is the soul of the body, as the body is the body of the soul.* As David writes:

> For you formed *my* inward parts;
>> you knitted *me* together in my mother's womb.
> I praise you, for *I* am fearfully and wonderfully made.
> Wonderful are your works;
>> *my* soul knows it very well.
> *My* frame was not hidden from you,
> when *I* was being made in secret,
>> intricately woven together in the depths of the
>> earth.
> Your eyes saw *my* unformed substance;
> in your book were written, every one of them,
>> the days that were formed for *me*
>> when as yet there was none of them. (Ps 139:13–16)

There is, then, no person or soul or spirit that has been created independently of the body and then placed in the body (or perhaps in the wrong body). As the Lord knit *my* body together in my mother's womb, "I was being made in secret." It is for this reason that the God-given sex of the body reveals God-ordained gender of the person.[61]

This understanding has profound and far-reaching implications, which Oliver O'Donovan expresses both clearly and compassionately:

> The sex into which we have been born (assuming that it is physiologically unambiguous) is given to us to be welcomed as a gift of God. The task of psychological maturity—for it is a moral task, and not merely an event which may or may not transpire—involves accepting this gift and learning to love it, even though we may have to acknowledge that it does not come to us without problems. Our task is to discern the possibilities for personal relationship which are given to us with this biological sex, and to seek to develop them in accordance with our individual vocations. … Responsibility in sexual development implies a responsibility to nature—to the ordered good of the bodily form which we have been given. And that implies that we must make the necessary distinction between the good of the bodily form as such and the various problems that it poses to us personally in our individual experience. This is a comment that applies not only to this very striking and unusually distressing problem, but to a whole range of other sexual problems too.[62]

So, while all kinds of things can and do go wrong with each and every one of us—both physiologically and psychologically, the Bible offers no support to the idea that one can actually be a man trapped in a woman's body or a woman trapped in a man's body. That may well be a person's subjective feeling, but it is not an objective fact.

This is not to deny that there are social or cultural elements to gender expression and gender roles. Nor is it to deny that a person's gender identity (i.e., how they perceive or desire themselves to be) may be at odds with their biological sex. The point is that, contrary to current gender theory, the true gender of the inner person is revealed by the sex of their outer body. Gender identity, therefore, needs to take its cues from and be guided by this fact. Sam Allberry puts it this way:

> Our culture says: Your psychology is your sexual identity—let your body be conformed to it.
>
> The Bible says: Your body is your sexual identity—let your mind be conformed to it.[63]

PROHIBITIONS AGAINST GENDER BENDING

Such an understanding helps us to see the rationale behind the Bible's condemnation of a number of behaviors that (in various ways) fall under the banner of gender bending.

The first of these behaviors is that of cross-dressing. This is addressed directly and unequivocally in Deuteronomy 22:5:

A woman shall not wear a man's garment, nor shall
a man put on a woman's cloak, for whoever does
these things is an abomination to the LORD your
God.

There can be little doubt that this text condemns
cross-dressing in the strongest possible terms. This is clear
from the use of the Hebrew word *to'evah* ("abomination"),
which means "detestable, repulsive or loathsome" and is
applied to any act that is "excluded by its very nature" or
is regarded as "dangerous."[64] It is thus the word applied
to various idolatrous practices (Deut 7:5; 13:14), homosexual intercourse (Lev 18:22; 20:13), and other violations
of either the created order or old covenant purity laws.[65]

But why should cross-dressing be seen in such terms?
Many commentators have assumed a link with either
homosexuality or pagan religion. This is possible, but there
is nothing in the immediate context to suggest such a connection. It is more likely, then, that "the wording of the
legislation goes beyond a cult setting to include any and
all circumstances of men dressing like women and vice
versa."[66] Thus, the nineteenth-century German commentators Carl Keil and Franz Delitzsch concluded:

The immediate design of this prohibition was not
to prevent licentiousness, or to oppose idolatrous
practices ... but to maintain the sanctity of that
distinction of the sexes which was established by

the creation of man and woman, and in relation to which Israel was not to sin.[67]

Consequently, as Peter Harland explains: "To dress after the manner of the opposite sex was to infringe the natural order of creation which divided humanity into male and female. That distinction was fundamental to human existence and could not be blurred in any way."[68] This is why the Lord regarded such blurring as an "abomination."

But what is the relevance of this text to new covenant Christians living in the twenty-first century? While care is needed in applying old covenant commands to later situations, the abiding ethical principles behind them can be readily discerned. It is not, then, as some have claimed, "doing a disservice to reasonable hermeneutics" to apply this verse to contemporary forms of transvestitism, certainly not to those who claim to be Christians.[69] Now as then, "this injunction seeks to preserve the order built into creation, specifically the fundamental distinction between male and female. For a person to wear anything associated with the opposite gender confuses one's sexual identity and blurs established boundaries."[70] This does not mean that all men (or all women) must dress alike, or that "unisex" items of clothing (like T-shirts or jeans) are inherently problematic. But it does warn us against intentional cross-dressing, particularly for the purpose of bending or disguising one's true sex.

The second of the behaviors that Scripture censures is sexual effeminacy; that is, a man playing the part of a woman (by being the "receiver") in homosexual inter-course. Those who engage in such a practice, and are finally unrepentant, are listed among those who will be excluded from the kingdom of God:

> Or do you not know that the unrighteous will not inherit the kingdom of God? Do not be deceived; neither fornicators, nor idolaters, nor adulterers, nor effeminate [*malakoi*], nor homosexuals [*arsenokoitai*], nor thieves, nor the covetous, nor drunkards, nor revilers, nor swindlers, will inherit the kingdom of God. (1 Cor 6:9–10 NASB)

Like his sexual ethics generally, the apostle Paul's assess-ment of homosexual behavior derives from the absolute prohibitions found in Leviticus 18:22 and 20:13, and so—like Deuteronomy 22:5—is ultimately grounded in the cre-ation theology of Genesis 1–3.[71] His use of the two distinct Greek terms highlighted above reveals that he is censuring all who participate in homosexual acts—whether actively or passively.[72] His reference to the "soft man" (*malokos*), therefore, is not aimed at victims of exploitative relation-ships or homosexual rape (as some have suggested), but at any man who actively feminizes himself by "being lain with 'as though a woman.'"[73]

Self-feminization for the purposes of homosexual sex is thus unambiguously condemned by Paul. However, given the semantic breadth of the term *malakoi* (and the fact that Paul could have used a more specific term if he wished to narrow its application),[74] it is also likely that he is censuring "those who engage in a process of feminization to erase further their masculine appearance and manner."[75] Consequently, if the practice of cross-dressing remains problematic for God's people (as Deut 22:5 indicates), and cross-gender identification is condemned here by Paul, then how much more would he have opposed hormonal and surgical transitioning?

The third of the behaviors that the Bible opposes is gender ambiguity; that is, the attempt to blur the lines between male and female by one's gender expression. This is Paul's chief concern in 1 Corinthians 11:2–16 and why he says:

> Every man who prays or prophesies with his head covered dishonors his head. But every woman who prays or prophesies with her head uncovered dishonors her head—it is the same as having her head shaved. … Judge for yourselves: Is it proper for a woman to pray to God with her head uncovered? Does not the very nature of things teach you that if a man has long hair, it is a disgrace to him, but that if a woman has long hair, it is her glory? For long hair is given to her as a covering. (1 Cor 11:4–5, 13–15 NIV)

Although there are a number of difficulties and obscurities in the passage in which these verses appear,[76] what is clear is that Paul desires both men and women in general, and husbands and wives in particular, to wholeheartedly

47

embrace and unambiguously express the gender distinctions with which we have been created, rather than to deny, diminish, or disguise them.[77] In the context of their corporate worship, this meant that men/husbands were not to cover their heads when praying or prophesying and that women/wives were to do the opposite—that is, cover their heads.[78]

The other dimension of Paul's concern with the gender blurring, if not gender exchanging, behavior of the Corinthians was their implicit rejection of the God-given order between husbands and wives, and the consequent dishonoring of one's head occasioned by their behavior— for example, a husband's dishonoring of Christ by covering his head and a wife's dishonoring of her husband by uncovering her head (vv. 4–5).[79]

How, then, does Paul's instruction apply to twenty-first-century Christians? While, in contemporary Western cultures, "there is no piece of clothing that functions as a cultural equivalent to the first-century Graeco-Roman head covering," this does not mean that there are no cultural symbols that send a similar message.[80] Taking the teaching of this passage seriously will necessarily impact the way Christian men and women "do gender"; that is, the way we present ourselves in terms of hair style, clothing choices and general demeanor. Although cultures differ, "in every culture there are certain kinds of adornment which become culturally acceptable norms of dress for men and women."[81] Our aim, then, is not to replicate first-century church practice, but to operate within the norms of our culture and to do so in such a way that we signal our recognition of both the God-given differences between men and woman and our grateful embrace of our own biologically-determined gender.

As we reflect further on the implications of the above passages for those with gender identity struggles, three things need to be appreciated. The first is that the moral commandments of the Bible "are not arbitrary decrees but correspond to the way the world is and will be."[82] Thus, the passages we've just considered, when rightly understood and applied (particularly in light of God's gospel mercies), call us back to creational norms and on towards creational ends. Put differently, both the precepts and prohibitions of Scripture show us what it means to work with the grain of creation toward the goal of new creation.[83] This is why Moses insists that the law of the Lord is "no empty word for you, but your very life" (Deut 32:47) and why John writes that "his commandments are not burdensome" (1 John 5:3).

Second, it is important to recognize that none of the three texts we have just examined suggest that those with genuine gender incongruence are culpable for their suffering. There is a biblical category of affliction that is clearly a consequence of humanity's sin but not necessarily, and certainly not always, a consequence of the afflicted person's own sin (e.g., John 9:1–3). Therefore, unlike willful, rebellious gender bending or deliberate, destructive gender erasing (which are certainly prohibited by such texts), the

49

experience of gender incongruence would appear to be largely a non-volitional, and to that extent a non-moral, condition.[84] It is also a deeply distressing one. Consequently, our first response to those who have to bear it ought to be compassion and care, not condemnation or criticism.

Third, the Bible's teaching certainly has implications for how we should respond to gender identity problems—whether our own or another's. There are right and wrong ways to address or manage all of life's challenges, including mental health battles like gender dysphoria. It therefore needs to be said that, as far as the Bible's teaching is concerned, trying to obliterate, disguise, or live at odds with one's God-given sex is contrary to God's will and against human good. Consequently, any attempt to do so is not only sinful but is unlikely to bring the relief that sufferers are seeking and may even bring them even greater distress in the longer term.[85]

THE SAVING AND SANCTIFYING POWER OF JESUS CHRIST

What then, according to Scripture, is the way forward? If not by transitioning, how should someone who experiences gender incongruence seek to bear their affliction? Here is where we need to understand the saving and sanctifying power of our Lord Jesus Christ and how it is applied by the Spirit to believers in the present age.

The first and fundamental thing to appreciate is that all those who confess Jesus as Lord and believe in their hearts that God raised him from the dead are justified from sin, brought to new birth by the Holy Spirit, and given a new identity as sons and daughters of the living God. "Therefore," writes Paul, "if anyone is in Christ, he is a new creation. The old has passed away; behold, the new has come" (2 Cor 5:17). Consequently, not only does the gift of divine acceptance provide the key to self-acceptance, but our union with Christ opens the door to a whole new self-understanding. We are no longer defined by our failures or our feelings. For as Paul writes elsewhere: "It is no longer I who live, but Christ who lives in me" (Gal 2:20a). In short, no Christian is what they once were (1 Cor 6:11). Christ has taken from us all that shamed and defiled us, all that crushed and condemned us, and made us "sharers with him in the gifts with which he has been endowed."[86] Due to the indwelling of his Spirit, Christ is in every believer and every believer is "in Christ" (John 14:16–20). Christians have truly been given new life (eternal life!) that we might be and become our true selves.

Second, new life leads to a new lifestyle. This is why all who are in Christ are called to "no longer live for themselves but for him who for their sake died and was raised" (2 Cor 5:15). This, however, does not mean that Christians experience the removal of all temptations and afflictions— not, at least, in this age. What it does mean is that there is a new power at work in us (that of the Holy Spirit), and so new possibilities open to us (choosing righteousness over sin). So, writes Paul, "let not sin therefore reign in your mortal body, to make you obey its passions" (Rom 6:12). The reason such resistance is now possible is because "our old self was crucified with him in order that the body of sin might be brought to nothing, so that we would no longer be enslaved to sin" (Rom 6:6). This call to walk in "newness of life" (Rom 6:4) has profound implications for every dimension of our existence, including what we do with and to our bodies. The Christian's body is now a temple of the Holy Spirit. "You are not your own," says Paul, "for you were bought with a price. So glorify God in your body" (1 Cor 6:19–20). A further implication of this exhortation is that all forms of self-harm are nothing less than a tragic defacing of that temple.

Third, among the vices of the old self that all believers are called to discard are covetousness and deception. I draw attention to these two particular sins because of their relevance to the subject at hand. As to the first, many who struggle with gender incongruence are sorely tempted to desire a body other than the one they have been given. That desire, to be frank, is a form of covetousness. Paul's advice is blunt: "Put to death, therefore, whatever belongs to your earthly nature: sexual immorality, impurity, lust, evil desires and covetousness, which is idolatry" (Col 3:5 NIV). As to the second, the aim of many who seek to transition genders is to "pass" as a member of the opposite sex. This is deception. Again, the apostle pulls no punches: "Do not lie to each other, since you have taken off your old self with its practices and have put on the new self, which is being renewed in knowledge in the image of its Creator" (Col 3:9–10 NIV). The implication of these injunctions is, therefore, clear: faithfulness to Christ cannot be separated from how a person manages their gender identity challenges.[87] Consequently, no Christian is at liberty to attempt to change their gender, and the desire to have a differently sexed body is a temptation that needs to be resisted.

Fourth, just as there are vices that believers are called to "put off," so there are virtues that we are called to "put on." Four are of special relevance to all who are called to bear the yoke of suffering over the long haul: endurance, patience, joy, and thanksgiving. Development of such Christlike characteristics is repeatedly encouraged in Scripture, but these four are brought together by the apostle Paul in his prayer for the Colossian Christians, asking that they would be

> strengthened with all power, according to [God's] glorious might, for all endurance and patience with joy; giving thanks to the Father, who has qualified you to share in the inheritance of the saints in light. (Col 1:11–12)

Endurance and patience are vital for sufferers of gender dysphoria, particularly for those whose cross-gender identification is strong and persistent. No one is helped by underplaying either the distress of such a condition or the force of the temptation to alleviate it in disobedient and self-destructive ways. However, resistance and obedience are possible, although much prayer is needed that strength be given to this end. Here is where a healthy perspective on the nature of the Christian life is vital, for it is "through many tribulations we must enter the kingdom of God" (Acts 14:22). Here also is where the importance of the biblical practice of lament is highlighted, for Scripture encourages us to pour out our sorrows and complaints before the Lord (e.g., Ps 102). On the positive side, joy and thanksgiving are also possible—if not for the affliction itself, for the sufficiency of God's grace (2 Cor 12:9) and the fruit that perseverance bears under the sovereign hand of God (Jas 1:2–4). It is in this way that God's children are able to rejoice in their sufferings (Rom 5:3–5).[88]

Fifth, at this point someone might ask, "But shouldn't we try to alleviate suffering wherever possible? And, if so, is there not an argument for relieving a gender dysphoric person's distress by bringing their body into alignment with their mind?" Traditional medical ethics would suggest not. The canons of sound medical practice have typically "ruled against surgical intervention into a living human body except to protect the functional integrity of that body when it was endangered by disease or injury."[89] For Christians, the biblical doctrines of creation, incarnation, and resurrection all support the view that "the physical structure of our human bodies is not something we are free to change without very careful thought."[90] What this means, as Dr. John Wyatt points out, is that we should only use medical and surgical technology "in a way which is appropriate to preserve and protect the original design, to maintain and preserve the creation order embodied in the structure of the human body."[91]

In the case of gender incongruence, it is the mind that is disordered, not the body. "SRS, therefore, is a 'category mistake'—it offers a surgical solution for psychological problems."[92] Furthermore, "SRS is a 'permanent,' effectively unchangeable, and often unsatisfying surgical attempt to change what may be only a temporary (i.e., psychotherapeutically changeable) psychological/psychiatric condition."[93] In other words, because the problem is in the mind and not the body, it should be treated with psychotherapy and not surgery. Moreover, it is becoming increasingly clear that surgical transitioning is likely to increase and prolong the experience of gender dysphoria for many. As one recent study has concluded: "Individuals diagnosed with gender incongruence who had received gender-affirming surgery were more likely to be treated for anxiety disorders compared with individuals diagnosed with gender incongruence who had not received gender-affirming surgery."[94] Consequently, any treatment of gender incongruence that seeks to relieve mental suffering by inflicting harm on an otherwise healthy body cannot be deemed ethical—either in principle or in practice.[95]

Sixth, battles with gender incongruence, whether long-term or short, should never be fought alone. Like all who suffer from a crippling disability, those who are afflicted by gender dysphoria are in great need of compassionate and practical support from others. This is one of the reasons why the risen Christ has given his followers the gift of brothers and sisters—not only to keep us accountable, but that we might bear one another's burdens. As Paul writes:

> Brothers and sisters, if someone is caught in a sin, you who live by the Spirit should restore that person gently. But watch yourselves, or you also may be tempted. Carry each other's burdens, and in this way you will fulfill the law of Christ. (Gal 6:1–2 NIV)

This text raises the important question: What counts as sin and what counts as a burden? In my view, the experience of gender incongruence falls most naturally in the latter category (burden). Mark Yarhouse is, therefore, right to argue that "there is a need for the church to be able to cope with the disclosure of gender dysphoria among those who experience it and have the courage to share what they are going through."[96] And not just cope, but embrace, love, understand, and protect. These precious brothers and sisters require our special care and must be surrounded by much emotional, spiritual, and practical support and prayer.

At the same time, and as we've already noted, there are ways of managing gender incongruence that, from a biblical standpoint, fall into the category of sin. What, then, will gentle restoration look like when such sin takes place? To answer this question responsibly in any given case, a range of factors will need to be taken into account: for example, whether the person is Christian or non-Christian, whether they are spiritually mature or spiritually immature, their level of intellectual and moral capacity, the severity and complexity of their dysphoria, and whether they have other physical or mental health issues. Nevertheless, in light of the clear direction that Scripture gives and the clear boundaries it draws, Yarhouse's advice—that some believers "may benefit from space to find ways to identify with aspects of the opposite sex, as a way to manage extreme discomfort"—ought not be followed.[97] All forms of intentional cross-gender identification are inappropriate for those in Christ. The fact that some of God's people desire such "space" does not mean it is beneficial for them. Repentance, then, will mean seeking to live consistently with one's God-given sex.

Furthermore, the good of the church community must also be considered. What message is being sent by a church that effectively encourages behavior that Scripture prohibits? What effect will this have on other members of Christ's body—particularly those who are vulnerable and impressionable? Paul's concern that "a little leaven leavens the whole lump of dough" (1 Cor 5:6) clearly has some application here. Having said that, and as we've also already noted, needlessly imposing rigid gender stereotypes (e.g., that all men must have crewcuts or all women must wear skirts) is not helpful either. While gender is not a spectrum, masculinity is a spectrum and femininity is a spectrum—that is, there is a range of faithful ways of being a man and a range of faithful ways of being a woman. Provided believers are operating and presenting themselves within accepted norms and cultural expectations for gender roles and gender expression, not all Christian men and women need to look, dress, and behave in precisely the same way.[98]

BODILY RESURRECTION
AND THE LIFE TO COME

The final piece of scriptural teaching relevant to our subject has to do with what is revealed about the nature of our resurrection bodies. Admittedly, there are all kinds of things we cannot know on this score (1 Cor 15:35–36). Nevertheless, in broad terms, the Bible affirms a principle of both continuity and transformation (1 Cor 15:42–44). That is, following the pattern of Jesus' own resurrection, it is these earthly bodies that will be raised (continuity), but with different qualities and capacities (transformation). As Paul says, Christ "will transform our lowly body to be like his glorious body" (Phil 3:21).

Curiously, the prospect of transformation has led some to speculate about the possibility of our being raised as either androgynous or monosexual or asexual beings. Given that our bodies are sexed in this world, and that the risen Jesus remains a man, it would require a very clear statement of Scripture to create the expectation that we will be raised as something other than eternally sexed (and therefore gendered) beings. But no such statement exists, and, despite occasional claims to the contrary, neither 1 Corinthians 6:13–15 nor Galatians 3:28 teaches any such thing. Indeed, the point of the first passage is that Christians ought not to engage in sexually immoral behavior because our bodies belong to Christ (1 Cor 6:13), are "members of Christ" (v. 15) and God intends to raise them (v. 14). And the point of the second passage (in particular, the statement that "there is no male and female, for you are all one in Christ Jesus") is that both male and female believers in Christ are equally God's children (Gal 3:26), have equally "put on Christ" (v. 27), and are equally Abraham's offspring and inheritors of all that God has promised them (v. 29).[99] In short, neither passage implies the elimination of sex/gender distinctions, either in this age or in the one to come.

The only passage that could possibly be thought to suggest such a possibility is Matthew 22:30 (and parallels), where Jesus says: "For in the resurrection neither do they marry nor are they given in marriage, but are like the angels." But while this passage clearly affirms that marriage belongs to this age only, it says nothing about the elimination of human sexual distinctions.[100] In fact, Jesus' choice of words in verse 30 implies quite the opposite: as Augustine rightly saw, "neither do they marry" can only refer to males and "nor are they given in marriage" can only refer to females.[101] Therefore, "far from saying that there will be no distinctions of gender in the new creation, Jesus said in essence that those who are male in heaven will not take a wife, nor will those who are female be given in marriage."[102]

Scripture, then, gives us no reason to doubt and every reason to believe that we will be resurrected not simply as embodied beings, but as sexed (and therefore gendered) beings. We will certainly be changed (1 Cor 15:51–52), but not changed from men or women into something else. Rather we will be changed from mortal to immortal, perishable to imperishable men and women (1 Cor 15:53–54).[103] Indeed, Paul's language in 1 Corinthians 15:53 could not be clearer: "For *this* perishable body must put on the imperishable, and *this* mortal body must put on immortality" (emphasis added). Reflecting on the import of these words, Matthew Mason comments as follows:

> *This* body, given to me by my Creator according to his original purpose, including its biological sex and the personal gender identity that entails, is the body that will rise on the last day—transformed, powerful, immortal, and glorious beyond my imagining.[104]

While the eternal purpose of our sex distinctions is yet to be fully disclosed, the suggestion that it has to do with the way in which humanity as male and female images the unity and distinction within the Trinity seems likely.[105] Whatever the case, "men and women will always be beings-in-relation, even when the business of marrying and procreating has been fulfilled."[106]

The glorious prospect of bodily resurrection has two implications. First, whatever kinds of dysphoria, disability, or disappointment we may have to deal with in this life, it matters what we do with and to the bodies God has given us (as we have seen). In fact, while we should be willing to spend and be spent in the cause of our Master, we are nonetheless to love our bodies. As Paul says, "no one ever hated his own flesh, but nourishes and cherishes it, just as Christ does the church" (Eph 5:29). Consequently, self-rejection and self-mutilation are not only tragic but also sinful. Those in Christ, therefore, must resist such temptations and instead fly to the throne of grace, where we can find "mercy and find grace to help in time of need" (Heb 4:16), and seek each other's assistance and encouragement that none of us "may be hardened by the deceitfulness of sin" (Heb 3:13).

Second, in the resurrection every form of disease and disorder, sickness and sadness will be healed and banished once and for all. Little wonder, then, that "we wait eagerly for our adoption to sonship, the redemption of our bodies" (Rom 8:23). Indeed, says Paul, "in this hope we have been saved" (Rom 8:24). What's more, so wonderful will be the glory revealed both to us and in us that the sufferings of this present time will not be worth comparing to it (Rom 8:18). This is good news for all of God's people, but particularly for those whose gender incongruence proves irresolvable in this life. Christians have a real hope that will not disappoint us. This is why we are called to wait for it with patience (Rom 8:25) and to fix our eyes not on what is seen and transient but on what is unseen and eternal (2 Cor 4:18).

5

CONCLUDING
THOUGHTS

H OW SHOULD WE think about gender incongruence and the distress it produces? In light of the Bible's teaching, and in the absence of any compelling evidence for regarding it as a type of intersex condition, genuine gender dysphoria is best regarded as a psychological disorder.[107] In other words, despite what is sometimes claimed, there is no reason (either biblical or scientific) to believe that a person can have either the brain or soul of one sex and the body of the other.[108] It may be a person's strong feeling or deeply held conviction, but it is not an objective fact. As one of the tragic effects of the fall, the gender dysphoric person is suffering from an affliction of the mind.

In and of itself, such a conclusion does little to remove or ameliorate the distress of those who suffer from a profound sense of gender incongruence. It does, however, lay some important foundations upon which to build a biblically informed, pastorally sensitive, and medically responsible therapeutic approach. It likewise provides a helpful interpretive grid through which we can make sense of the various social, political, and ideological changes going on around us. For not only is the basic claim of transgender ideology unsustainable, but the goal of transitioning is unrealizable. "Transgendered men do not become women, nor do transgendered women become men."[109] As Dr. Paul McHugh writes, the best they can ever hope to become is "counterfeits or impersonators of the sex with which they 'identify.' "[110]

What, then, is our message to those who have sought to transition—socially, hormonally, or surgically?

First, they need to come to Jesus and come just as they are. This means that in our evangelism we must not let the temporary overshadow the eternal. The greatest need of those who experience gender dysphoria or identify as transgender or have undergone SRS is not for their identity issues to be resolved (as wonderful as that would be), or their attempts at transitioning to be reversed (which may not be entirely possible), but to be reconciled to God and adopted as his children. In other words, like the rest of us, the gender confused need the gospel of Jesus Christ. For every human being has been created through and for Jesus Christ (Col 1:16), and will therefore be restless, as Augustine said, unless and until they find their rest in him. But rest is precisely what Jesus promises to all who come to him in faith (Matt 11:28)—irrespective of their past sins or present burdens. This is the hope of the gospel: that true life, lasting peace, and eternal comfort can be found in Jesus Christ.

Second, while we are all invited to come to Jesus as we are, he is not content to leave any of us as we are. His goal is to restore us into his image and teach us to discern and do the will of God (Rom 12:2). For the reasons we've seen, this will necessarily entail living, as far as is possible, in conformity with our God-given sex. For those who have gone down the path of transitioning, this will mean ceasing CHT, cross-dressing, and other forms of cross-gender identification. Some surgical steps may, of course, be irreversible. If so, as Russell Moore explains, the person may need to see themselves akin to a biblical eunuch (of the man-made variety); that is, as one wounded physically by a past action but awaiting wholeness in the resurrection.[111] Whatever the case, sensitive pastoral care (if not appropriate medical care also) and strong congregational support will be essential for anyone who, in obedience to Christ, is seeking to de-transition.

Finally, how should Christians respond to the transgender revolution that is currently sweeping the Western world?

If we truly love our neighbors, we will not withdraw from the public square, particularly if we understand the way in which "today's uncontested folly becomes tomorrow's accepted wisdom."[112] Therefore we must not only pray fervently for our world but, as part of our prophetic task, take up our apologetic responsibility to expose the corrupt foundations and calamitous effects of contemporary gender ideology. In addition to that, and where possible, we will work politically for ways of treating gender incongruence that don't normalize a psychological disorder or incentivize self-harm, for public policies that don't perpetuate gender confusion and facilitate social contagion, and for truly safer school programs that protect the dignity and interests of *all* children. As in our evangelism, engaging at this level will not always make us popular; indeed it may see some of us persecuted, prosecuted, and even imprisoned. But if we're going to bring the liberating truth of Christ to a lost and confused culture, then, as Albert Mohler reminds us, we cannot be silent.[113] Our calling as Christ's followers, as has often been said, is to present the truth with compassion but without compromise. May the Spirit of God enable us for such a task, for the love of Christ demands no less from us.

Acknowledgments

T HE SERIES Questions for Restless Minds is produced
by the Christ on Campus Initiative, under the steward-
ship of the editorial board of D. A. Carson (senior editor),
Douglas Sweeney, Graham Cole, Dana Harris, Thomas
McCall, Geoffrey Fulkerson, and Scott Manetsch. The editorial board recognizes with gratitude the many outstand-
ing evangelical authors who have contributed to this series,
as well as the sponsorship of Trinity Evangelical Divinity
School (Deerfield, Illinois), and the financial support of
the MAC Foundation and the Carl F. H. Henry Center
for Theological Understanding. The editors also wish to
thank Christopher Gow, who created the study questions
accompanying each book, and Todd Hains, our editor
at Lexham Press. May God alone receive the glory for
this endeavor!

Study Guide Questions

1. After reading this book, what are your initial thoughts and feelings? What about it did you find challenging? What did you find encouraging or hopeful?

2. What are some of the different ways of defining gender represented in this book? Smith notes that many of these ways of thinking about gender are new and innovative. How does he explain the emergence of these new ways of thinking (19)?

3. Smith notes on page 17 that one effect of the changes in our culture is that rather than ask, "Who am I?" people ask, "What do I identify as?" What difference does this make?

4. Genesis 1 refers to Adam and Eve using the Hebrew words for "male" and "female," (which are words also used for animals) whereas Genesis 2 uses the words for "man" and

"woman" (which are words unique to humans). Why does Smith emphasize this shift in language (35)? What point is he making about the relationship between gender and sexuality?

5. In chapter 4, Smith articulates a biblical-theological understanding of gender and sexuality. Take a moment to review his points and the Scripture he cites. How would you briefly sketch an outline of the Bible's teaching on these matters in terms of creation, fall, redemption in Christ, and resurrection to come?

6. Have you considered your own relationship to your gender as an aspect of your discipleship to Jesus? Personally, does this sketch of the Bible's teaching on sexuality and gender challenge your self-understanding, refocus your confidence in the redemption brought by Christ, or present a call to new forms of discipleship?

7. What does Smith say should be a Christian's first response to someone who is dealing with gender incongruence (66)? What are a few specific ways that you as an individual, small group, or congregation can better love, evangelize, and disciple people who experience gender incongruence in your community (e.g., prayer, outreach, compassionate service, further study)?

For Further Reading

Anderson, Ryan T. *When Harry Became Sally: Responding to the Transgender Moment*. Encounter Books, 2018.

Although Anderson writes as a convinced Catholic, *When Harry Became Sally* is not an explicitly Christian book. It is, nonetheless, an important and penetrating evaluation of the transgender movement that skilfully brings together insights from the fields of biology, psychology, sociology, and philosophy. Moreover, by introducing readers to some of the growing number of "detransitioners," Anderson also reveals that the media's excessively positive portrayal of gender transitioning is, at best, only part of the story. Of particular value is Anderson's highlighting of the various contradictions that beset trans ideology—for example, its reliance on rigid sex stereotypes along with an insistence that gender is a social construct; its assumption that subjective identity deserves absolute respect, whereas objective embodiment does not; its commitment to people

73

finding their own truth, while denying them freedom to dissent from trans orthodoxy. The book concludes with an important chapter on "Policy in the Common Interest" that is of particular relevance to American readers.

Branch, J. Alan. *Affirming God's Image: Addressing the Transgender Question with Science and Scripture.* Lexham Press, 2018.

With the goal of joining "conviction and compassion in an evaluation of transgenderism," Branch's book is a wide-ranging investigation of the social, historical, theological, ethical, medical, and pastoral dimensions of the transgender phenomenon. His basic conviction is that a transgender identity is one that is "rooted in multiple causes and is completely inconsistent with Christian ethics" (4). However, because people do not choose to experience gender incongruence, he is also concerned that "a Christian response should always be expressed with a tone of mercy" (130). True to the word *science* in the subtitle, Branch includes four carefully researched chapters on "Genetics and Transgenderism" (chapter 4), "The Brain and Transgenderism" (chapter 5), "Hormonal Treatment of Gender Dysphoria" (chapter 6), and "Gender Reassignment Surgery" (chapter 7). In his third chapter ("Scripture and Transgenderism"), Branch examines the meaning of humanity's creation as male and female, the impact of the fall on sex, and the importance of gender-distinctions (e.g., Deut 22:5) and sex-based roles (e.g., Eph 5:21–33; Col 3:18–21; 1 Pet 3:1–7). His conclusion is that "the New Testament offers no option for transgender behaviour as a legitimate form of sexual expression" (52).

Gagnon, Robert J. *The Bible and Homosexual Practice.* Abingdon, 2002.

Although nearly two decades old, the thoroughness of Robert Gagnon's analysis of the biblical texts relating to homosexuality (and also transsexuality) has yet to be surpassed. Gagnon also addresses sexual issues discussed in the related literature of intertestamental Judaism and makes extensive reference to both biblical and extrabiblical material. Rigorously engaging scholars and historians of all persuasions, Gagnon demonstrates why attempts to classify the Bible's rejection of same-sex intercourse as irrelevant for our contemporary context fail to do justice to the biblical texts and also to current scientific data. This work is relevant to our subject because it contains treatments of a number of the texts we've examined (e.g., Gen 1–3; Deut 22:5; and the meaning of *malakoi* in 1 Cor 6:9), because it explores some possible links between homosexuality and transsexuality, and finally because it provides a model of responsible, scholarly exegesis.

James, Sharon. *Gender Ideology: What Do Christians Need to Know?* Christian Focus Publications, 2019.

Gender Ideology provides a critical analysis of contemporary gender theory and the belief that "gender identity" refers "to each person's deeply felt internal and individual experience of gender, which may or may not correspond with the sex assigned at birth" (38). Following chapters on "The Global Sexual Revolution" and "'Can we really Change Sex?' and other FAQs," chapter 3 critiques some of the "false claims" of gender theory, as well as the "misleading vocabulary" it generates. After answering the question, "Where Did 'Gender Theory' Come From?," chapter 5 explores some important biblical perspectives. Of particular value is James's insight that "God specifically designs and determines our body. It reflects His intent" (78). She also highlights the implications of Jesus' resurrection and his promise to raise us bodily: "When we disparage the physical body, we disparage Christ" (75). The book's penultimate chapter includes a helpful discussion of both child-onset gender dysphoria and rapid-onset gender dysphoria. The final chapter convincingly argues that gender theory is opposed to human flourishing.

Kuby, Gabrielle. *The Global Sexual Revolution: Destruction of Freedom in the Name of Freedom.* Translated by James Patrick Kirchner. LifeSite, 2015.

This courageous book provides a detailed historical, philosophical, and sociological survey of the rapid advance of the LGBT agenda, the devastating effects of pornography and sex-education, the assault on freedom of speech and religious liberty, the corruption of language, and the destabilization of the family. The net effect of these revolutionary developments is the dissolution of the identity of man and woman, the deregulation of sexual norms, and the free rein of polymorphous urges that have no ultimate meaning. From the movement's trailblazers to the post-Obergefell landscape, Gabrielle Kuby documents in detail how successive phases of the sexual revolution are slowly gripping the world in a stranglehold. The book, however, is not without hope. "There is resistance," writes Kuby, "and there is successful resistance. Around the world, Christian churches, NGOs, individuals and institutions are working for a culture that respects the dignity of the human person and fights for life, marriage and family" (258). What's more, "Christians know that the story will come out well" (278).

Mayer, Lawrence S. and Paul R. McHugh. "Sexuality and Gender: Findings from the Biological, Psychological, and Social Sciences." *The New Atlantis* 50 (Fall 2016): http://www.thenewatlantis.com/docLib/20160819_TNA 50SexualityandGender.pdf

This report, written by Dr. Lawrence Mayer, an epidemiologist trained in psychiatry, and Dr. Paul R. McHugh, one of the most important American psychiatrists of the last half-century, presents a careful summary and an up-to-date explanation of research from the biological, psychological, and social sciences in relation to the questions of sexual orientation and gender identity. The report reveals that many of the most frequently heard claims about sexuality and gender are not supported by scientific evidence. The report also has a special focus on the higher rates of mental health problems among LGBT populations and questions the scientific basis of trends in the treatment of children who do not identify with their biological sex. The report helpfully highlights the fact that "only a minority of children who experience cross-gender identification will continue to do so into adolescence or adulthood," as well as arguing that there is "little scientific evidence for the therapeutic value of interventions that delay puberty or modify the secondary sex characteristics of adolescents" (9).

O'Donovan, Oliver, "Transsexualism and Christian Marriage." *Journal of Religious Ethics* 11.1 (1983): 135–62.

This carefully argued account of the implications of transsexualism for marriage sets out the main theological objections to gender transitioning. Oliver O'Donovan's foundational argument is that it is impossible to be born into the "wrong body" because there is no pre-existing male or female soul that enters the body at birth. Consequently, sex reassignment surgery goes beyond the bounds of what is legitimate for humans to do with their God-given bodies. Nonetheless, he considers two cases against this conclusion. The *psychological case* argues that since biological sexuality cannot be considered on its own, the transsexual should be seen as ambiguously sexed. This, however, requires an overriding of the objective reality of the body. The *social case* argues that public acceptance of a transsexual's gender does not immediately depend on their "real" sex. This, however, requires the public affirmation of an illusion. As neither the psychological case nor the social case is persuasive, O'Donovan's theological objections to gender transitioning (in general) and transsexual marriage (in particular) remain.

Roberts, Vaughan. *Transgender*. The Good Book Company, 2016.

This short book (74 pages) supplies readers with a masterful but accessible introduction to the transgender phenomenon, as well as providing Christians with a starting point for constructive discussions both inside and outside the church. After surveying the main ingredients of the biblical-Christian worldview, Vaughan Roberts skilfully applies the Bible's teaching to the many complex questions surrounding the issue of gender identity. He does this not only with love and compassion for sufferers of gender dysphoria, but with an awareness that we live in a world of conflicting values that requires Christians to be clear-minded and courageous. Roberts's book serves as a very useful primer both for individuals struggling with personal gender questions as well as for anyone confused by the current cultural trends.

Shrier, Abigail. *Irreversible Damage: The Transgender Craze Seducing Our Daughters*. Regnery Publishing, 2020.

Why is it that in the last decade gender incongruence has shifted from being a rare condition, that almost exclusively afflicted young boys, to an epidemic among teenage girls? The answer, writes journalist Abigail Shrier, has little to do with "traditional gender dysphoria," and "everything to do with our cultural frailty" (xxiii). *Irreversible Damage* begins by introducing us to several teenage girls who suddenly came out as transgender after having been exposed to transition stories. Shrier then explores Lisa Littman's 2018 work on Rapid Onset Gender Dysphoria and her "peer contagion" hypothesis. Along the way, she not only interviews many of the girls' bewildered parents, but also the counsellors, doctors, and online "influencers" who encourage and enable gender transitioning. Critics of the so called gender-affirming model of care—e.g., Kenneth Zucker, Ray Blanchard, J. Michael Bailey, Lisa Marchiano, and Paul McHugh—are also heard, as are the voices of "detransitioners": those who deeply regret having undergone "treatments" that have rendered them permanently disfigured and infertile. This book is a must-read for anyone concerned for the welfare of children.

Sprinkle, Preston. *Embodied: Transgender Identities, the Church and What the Bible Has to Say.* David C Cook, 2021.

Embodied not only addresses the cultural, medical, psychological, and social angles of the transgender phenomenon, but also contains several chapters of valuable biblical exposition and rigorous theological exploration. Nevertheless, the work is set in a decidedly pastoral frame—beginning with a chapter on "People" and ending with a chapter on "Outrageous Love." In the early part of the book,

Sprinkle defines key terms—notably, *sex, gender, gender identity,* and *gender role*—before answering the question, "What Does it Mean to be Trans*?" Theologically, he starts by noting that "we bear God's image as male and female" (67) and concludes that the Bible writers view Genesis 1–2 as normative. The book also addresses the following: "Gender Stereotypes" (chapter 5), the biblical teaching on eunuchs (chapter 6), intersex conditions (chapter 7), and the possibility of having a male brain in a female body (chapter 8) or a female soul in a male body (chapter 9). The final section addresses rapid-onset gender dysphoria (chapter 10), transitioning and discipleship (chapter 11), pronouns, bathrooms, and sleeping spaces (chapter 12), and is completed by a wise and compassionate appendix on "Suicidality and Trans* People."

Walker, Andrew T. *God and the Transgender Debate: What Does the Bible Actually Say About Gender Identity?* The Good Book Company, 2017.

With gospel-minded clarity and Christ-like care, Andrew Walker deftly navigates a path between the folly of affirming transgenderism and the cruelty of dismissing the distress of those who experience gender incongruence. After a number of introductory chapters, explaining "How We Got to Where We Are" and where "here" is, Walker steps us through the Bible's story line and applies it along the way. In so doing, he shows why the gospel of Jesus Christ is good news for the transgendered and gender dysphoric, and how Scripture equips the church for the good work of loving and bearing witness to the LGBTQ community. The book also contains an important chapter on "Speaking to Children" (chapter 11), as well as a valuable "Tough Questions" section (chapter 12)—dealing with everything from restrooms to pronouns.

Yarhouse, Mark A. *Understanding Gender Dysphoria: Navigating Transgender Issues in a Changing Culture.* IVP, 2015.

In *Understanding Gender Dysphoria*, Mark Yarhouse (a professor of psychology and licensed psychologist) offers a Christian perspective on transgender issues (generally) and gender dysphoria (particularly). Addressing questions of causation, phenomenology, prevalence, prevention, and treatment, Yarhouse engages with the latest scientific research in chapters 3 to 5. The most important section of the book, however, is chapter 2, "A Christian Perspective on Gender Dysphoria." Here Yarhouse examines "the four acts of the biblical drama: *creation, fall, redemption* and *glorification*" (35) and then outlines "three different frameworks for understanding gender identity concerns" (46): integrity, disability, and diversity. The first two frameworks effectively combine the doctrines of creation and fall. The third approaches things from the perspective of the current "sociocultural context" in the West, which sees transgenderism "as something to be celebrated, honored, or revered" (50). While cautious about this framework (although, in my view, not cautious enough), Yarhouse sees it as having something important to teach us because it addresses questions of identity, meaning and acceptance, and thus highlights the need for Christians to come alongside those who are trying to resolve questions and concerns about their gender identity.

Notes

1. The new house rules can be found here: https://rules.house.gov/sites/democrats.rules.house.gov/files/BILLS-117hresPIH-hres5.pdf.

2. Hayley Dixon, "Policy tells midwives to use terms such as 'chestfeeding' and 'human milk,'" *The Sydney Morning Herald* (February 10, 2021): https://www.smh.com.au/world/europe/new-policy-tells-midwives-to-stop-using-terms-such-as-breastfeeding-and-breastmilk-20210210-p571b7.html.

3. "Brighton NHS Trust introduces new trans-friendly terms," *BBC News* (February 10, 2021): https://www.bbc.com/news/uk-england-sussex-56007728.

4. Karl Quinn, "'Transphobic' website puts Melbourne University academics at odds," *The Age* (February 25, 2021): https://www.theage.com.au/lifestyle/gender/transphobic-website-puts-melbourne-university-academics-at-odds-20210225-p575u4.html. The website established

by Lawford-Smith, "No conflict, they said," can be found at https://www.noconflicttheysaid.org.

5. For example, Russell Moore, "The Transgender Revolution and the Rubble of Empty Promises," *The Gospel Coalition* (June 6, 2017): https://www.thegospelcoalition.org/article/transgender-revolution-and-rubble-of-empty-promises.

6. That is, a man who has socially, hormonally, and surgically transitioned to become (or, at least, appear to become) a woman—otherwise known as an MTF (male to female).

7. Although the term "assigned sex" is increasingly being used, this language is problematic. Sex is not assigned but recognized or identified. Even when faced with an intersex condition, the doctor's task is to discover or clarify the child's sex, not to create or impose it.

8. J. A. Simpson and E. S. C. Weiner, eds., *Oxford English Dictionary* (Clarendon, 1989). However, it is important to note that *distinguishing* gender from sex is not the same as *disconnecting* gender from sex. This has been a more recent development.

9. Cisgender, however, is something of a loaded term, for it was coined and is often employed as a way of normalizing transgender experience. In other words, it suggests that it is just as natural for a person's gender identity to land on the *other side* of their sex, as it is for it to land on the *same side*.

10. *DSM*-V, 2013. *DSM* stands for the *Diagnostic and Statistical Manual of Mental Disorders*, which is published by the American Psychiatric Association.

11. Needless to say, this has been a highly controversial change and is regarded by some psychiatrists as an "abrogation of professional responsibility in the interest of political correctness." Richard B. Corradi, "Psychiatry Professor: 'Transgenderism' Is Mass Hysteria Similar to 1980s-Era Junk Science," *The Federalist* (November 17, 2016): http://thefederalist.com/2016/11/17/psychiatry-professor-transgenderism-mass-hysteria-similar-1980s-era-junk-science.

12. Interestingly, even the Intersex Society of North America is opposed to the idea that intersex people constitute a third gender on pragmatic grounds. See http://www.isna.org/faq/third-gender.

13. In deference to them, and for the reason given above (i.e., that Intersex covers a range of *biologically* based DSDs), I will use the LGBTQ+ acronym in this book. As is generally understood, L stands for "lesbian," G for "gay," B for "bi-sexual" and T for "transgender." Q normally stands for "queer," although it sometimes doubles up to cover "questioning" as well. The letter A—for "asexual"— is also becoming increasingly common. It can also double up for "all" (i.e., for someone who is an

LGBTQ ally). Further letters are sometimes added, but to keep the acronym manageable, these are often covered by " +."

14. The older term *transsexual* is still sometimes used of and by those who seek medical assistance to transition. Increasingly, however, it is regarded as outdated.

15. In philosophical terms, this speaks of the triumph of existentialism over essentialism. For in essentialist thought, *essence precedes existence* (i.e., what you are determines what you do, being determines act). But in existentialist thought, *existence precedes essence* (i.e., what you do determines what you are, act determines being). When linked with the postmodern "turn to the subject," this shift opens the door not only to transgenderism (identifying as a gender contrary to one's body), but to transracialism (identifying as a race contrary to one's ethnicity), transableism (identifying as disabled contrary to one's ability), and transspeciesism (identifying as a species contrary to one's DNA). All such identifications take the notion that "truth is subjectivity" to a place Søren Kierkegaard (who coined the phrase) never intended or imagined. For a recent defense of the thesis that the "considerations that support transgenderism extend to transracialism," see Rebecca Tuvel, "In Defense of Transracialism," *Hypatia* 32.2 (2017): 263–78.

16. See "Rin's Gender Dictionary A–Z," *Tumblr.com*, https://what-the-heck-gender-am-i.tumblr.com /genderdictionary%20.

17. Sarah Marsh and *Guardian* readers, "The gender-fluid generation: young people on being male, female or non-binary," *The Guardian* (March 23, 2016), https://www.theguardian.com/comment isfree/2016/mar/23/gender-fluid-generation -young-people-male-female-trans.

18. Marsh, "The gender-fluid generation."

19. Nick Duffy, "California Adopts Self-ID Gender Recognition Law," *Pink News* (January 3, 2019), https://www.pinknews.co.uk/2019/01/03 /california-gender-self-id.

20. This was the verdict of a 2014 *Time* magazine cover story. See Katy Steinmetz, "The Transgender Tipping Point," *Time* (May 29, 2014), http://time .com/135480/transgender-tipping-point.

21. The series, which premiered on July 11, 2013, features a black transgender character played by transwoman (i.e., MTF), actor Laverne Cox.

22. For an in-depth and insightful treatment of the historical antecedents that have led to the transgender revolution, see Carl R. Trueman, *The Rise and Triumph of the Modern Self: Cultural Amnesia, Expressive Individualism, and the Road to Sexual Revolution* (Crossway, 2020).

23. Simone de Beauvoir, *The Second Sex*, trans. and ed. H.M. Parshley (Picador, 1988), 295. First published in French as *Le Deuxième Sexe* (1949).

24. For a more comprehensive account of the many connections and conflicts between feminism, gay and lesbian studies, queer theory, and trans ideology, see Patricia Elliot, *Debates in Transgender, Queer, and Feminist Theory: Contested Sites* (Routledge, 2016); also Talia M. Bettcher, "Feminist Perspectives on Trans Issues," *Stanford Encyclopedia of Philosophy* (January 8, 2014), https://plato.stanford.edu/archives/spr2014/entries/feminism-trans.

25. Despite claims to the contrary, there is no clear or consistent evidence that gender identity is determined by microstructures in the brain. As Lawrence Mayer and Paul McHugh write, "The current studies on associations between brain structure and transgender identity are small, methodologically limited, inconclusive, and sometimes contradictory. Even if they were more methodologically reliable, they would be insufficient to demonstrate that brain structure is a cause, rather than an effect, of the gender-identity behavior." Lawrence S. Mayer and Paul R. McHugh, "Sexuality and Gender: Findings from the Biological, Psychological, and Social Sciences," *The New Atlantis*, 50 (Fall 2016), 104: http://www.thenewatlantis.com/docLib/20160819_TNA50SexualityandGender.pdf.

26. Preston Sprinkle, *Embodied: Transgender Identities, the Church and What the Bible Has to Say* (David C Cook, 2021), 33.

27. Lily Edelstein, "Sexual fluidity: Living a label-free life," *ABC News* (February 20, 2016), http://www.abc.net.au/news/2016-02-20/sexual-fluidity-label-free-life/7162884.

28. Judith Butler, "Imitation and Gender Insubordination," D. Fuss, ed., *Inside/Out: Lesbian Theories, Gay Theories* (Routledge, 1991), 13.

29. Judith Butler, "Preface (1999)," in *Gender Trouble: Feminism and the Subversion of Identity* (Routledge, 2006), xxiv.

30. Butler, "Preface (1999)," 9–10.

31. Virginia Ramey Mollenkott, "Gender Diversity and Christian Community," *The Other Side* 37/3 (May–June 2001), http://www.transfaithonline.org/articles/other/tos/genderdiversity.

32. Virginia Ramey Mollenkott, *Omnigender: A Trans-Religious Approach* (Pilgrim, 2007), 167.

33. Mollenkott, *Omnigender*, 8.

34. "Dr David Mackereth: Trans pronouns 'denial of obvious truth,'" *BBC News* (July 10, 2019), https://www.bbc.com/news/uk-england-birmingham-48937805.

35. Employment Judge Perry, "Dr David Mackereth v The Department for Work and Pensions and Advanced Personnel Management Group

(UK) Ltd: 1304602/2018" (September 26, 2019), https://christianconcern.com/wp-content/uploads/2018/10/CC-Resource-Judgment-Mackereth-DWP-Others-ET-191002.pdf.

36. John Bowden, "GOP senators question Amazon on removal of book about 'transgender moment,'" *The Hill* (March 3, 2021), https://thehill.com/policy/technology/541082-gop-senators-question-amazon-on-removal-of-book-about-transgender-moment.

37. Ryan T. Anderson, "When Amazon Erased My Book," *First Things* (February 23, 2021), https://www.firstthings.com/web-exclusives/2021/02/when-amazon-erased-my-book.

38. "Parliament of Victoria: Change or Suppression (Conversion) Practices Prohibition Bill 2020," https://content.legislation.vic.gov.au/sites/default/files/2020-12/591143bab1.pdf.

39. Neil Foster, "Victoria's Conversion Practices Bill is as bad as they say it is," *Law and Religion Australia* (January 15, 2021), https://lawandreligionaustralia.blog/2021/01/15/victorias-conversion-practices-bill-is-as-bad-as-they-say-it-is/#implications-unlawfulness.

40. "Change or Suppression (Conversion) Practices Prohibition Bill 2020: Introduction Print: Explanatory Memorandum," https://content.legislation.vic.gov.au/sites/default/files/bills/591143exi1.pdf.

41. Frank Bruni, "The Republicans' Gay Freakout," *New York Times* (April 2, 2016), http://www .nytimes.com/2016/04/03/opinion/sunday/the -republicans-gay-freakout.html?_r=0.

42. For example, the December 2020 court ruling against the treatment of British youth at the gender-identity clinic at the Tavistock Hospital, London (see "The judgment in Keira Bell's case upsets trans groups," *The Economist* (December 1, 2020), https://www.economist.com/britain/2020 /12/01/the-judgment-in-keira-bells-case-upsets -trans-groups.

43. Others (both Christian and non-Christian) have sought to address this latter need. I refer readers to the following works: R. Albert Mohler Jr., *The Gathering Storm Secularism, Culture, and the Church* (Nelson Books, 2020); Gabrielle Kuby, *The Global Sexual Revolution: Destruction of Freedom in the Name of Freedom*, trans. James Patrick Kirchner. (LifeSite, 2015). (First published in German as *Die globale sexuelle Revolution: Zerstörung der Freiheit im Namen der Freiheit* (Fe-Medienverlags Gmbh, 2012); Ryan T. Anderson, *When Harry Became Sally: Responding to the Transgender Moment* (Encounter Books, 2018); Abigail Shrier, *Irreversible Damage: The Transgender Craze Seducing Our Daughters* (Regnery, 2020); Rod Dreher, *Live Not by Lies: A Manuel for Christian Dissidents* (Sentinel, 2020).

44. This, it is important to say, does not mean that someone born with a DSD is "more fallen" than others.
Rather, their particular condition is simply one of the
ways (albeit a very significant one) that the fall has
impacted their body. Nevertheless, there are many
other kinds of disorder that affect the bodies of the
children of Adam, and all of our bodies are subject to
disease, deterioration, and death.

45. Michelle A. Cretella, Quentin Van Meter and
Paul McHugh, "Gender Identity Harms Children,"
American College of Pediatricians (August 17, 2016),
https://www.acpeds.org/the-college-speaks
/position-statements/gender-ideology-harms
-children.

46. There is some debate about which conditions are
rightly categorized as Intersex. If the category
is restricted to those conditions in which chro-
mosomal sex is inconsistent with phenotypic
(e.g., genital) sex, or in which the phenotype is
not classifiable as either male or female, then the
true prevalence of intersex is about 0.018 percent.
See Leonard Sax, "How common is Intersex? A
response to Anne Fausto-Sterling," *The Journal of
Sex Research* 39.3 (2002): 174–78.

47. As to the view that Adam was an androgyne (i.e., a
mix of both male and female) prior to God bringing forth Eve from his side, two things need to be
said. First, if it were true, God deemed it "not good"

and, having remedied it, made it irrelevant from that point on. Second, every indicator in the text of Genesis tells against it. Adam, after Eve's creation, remains Adam (minus a rib!) and Eve is called woman (*'ishshah*) precisely because she was taken out of man (*'ish*). In other words, Adam was a man (*'ish*) before and after Eve's creation.

48. Contrary to the claims of an increasing number of queer parents. See, for example, Katherine D. M. Clover, "Please Stop Calling My Child 'Little Man,'" *Ravishly* (March 18, 2016), http://www.ravishly .com/2016/03/16/please-stop-calling-my-child -little-man.

49. I am not suggesting, however, that biology alone dictates *how* a person expresses their gender (i.e., manhood) or performs a gender role (i.e., mother-hood). For the Christian, this will be determined by the word of God and by the application of godly wisdom to our personal circumstances and to our particular cultural context.

50. I maintain this despite claims that biological men will be able to receive womb transplants and bear children within a decade. See Doug Mainwar-ing, "Health experts: 'Transgender' men will bear children within next decade," *Life Site News* (July 4, 2017), https://www.lifesitenews.com/news/health -experts-transgender-men-will-bear-children -within-next-decade.

51. Both the Hebrew word *saris* and the Greek word *eunouchos* can refer either to a court officer (Gen 39:1) or to a castrated male (Isa 56:3) or to one who was both (possibly Acts 8:27).

52. See, for example, D. A. Carson, "Matthew," F. E. Gaebelein, ed., *The Expositor's Bible Commentary* Vol. 8 (Regency, 1984), 419; L. L. Morris, *The Gospel According to Matthew* (Eerdmans, 1992), 485–86; R. T. France, *The Gospel According to Matthew*, NICNT (Eerdmans, 2007), 725.

53. See F. P. Retief and J. F. G. Cilliers, "Congenital Eunuchism and Favorinus," *SAMJ* 93.1 (January 2003): 73–76.

54. This is a much-contested question. See, for example, Shaun Tougher, *The Eunuch in Byzantine History and Society* (Routledge, 2008); Kathryn M. Ringrose, "Eunuchs in Historical Perspective," *History Compass* 5.2 (March 2007): 495–506; Ringrose, *The Perfect Servant: Eunuchs and the Social Construction of Gender in Byzantium* (University of Chicago Press, 2003); Mathew Kuefler, *The Manly Eunuch: Masculinity, Gender Ambiguity and Christian Ideology in Late Antiquity* (University of Chicago Press, 2001).

55. Contrary to the suggestion of Megan K. de Franza, *Sex Difference in Christian Theology: Male, Female, and Intersex in the Image of God* (Eerdmans, 2015), 66.

56. For example, "'Inner man,' 'spirit,' 'soul,' 'mind,' 'heart,'—all do duty for the incorporeal part of man and different functions thereof. 'Outer man,' 'flesh,' 'body,' 'members,' 'mouth,' 'face,' and several metaphors do similar duty for the corporeal part of man." See Robert H. Gundry, *Sōma in Biblical Theology: With Emphasis on Pauline Anthropology* (Zondervan, 1987), 156.

57. Admittedly, there are two texts that suggest a distinction between "soul" and "spirit" (1 Thess 5:23; Heb 4:12), which some see as evidence for a trichotomous or tripartite view. However these texts might best be interpreted, they do not disturb the general, two-fold distinction between the inner and outer person.

58. Some passages of Scripture (for example, Matt 26:41; 1 Cor 5:5) employ a parallel contrast between "flesh" (Greek, *sarx*) and "spirit" (*pneuma*).

59. John W. Cooper, *Body, Soul, and Life Everlasting: Biblical Anthropology and the Monism-Dualism Debate* (Eerdmans, 1989), 78.

60. Cooper, *Body, Soul, and Life Everlasting,* 78.

61. See further Sprinkle, *Embodied,* 145–54.

62. Oliver O'Donovan, *Begotten or Made?* (OUP, 1984), 28–29.

63. Cited in Vaughan Roberts, *Transgender* (The Good Book Company, 2016), 43.

64. Ernst Jenni and Claus Westermann, *Theological Lexicon of the Old Testament* (Hendrickson, 1997), 1429. See also Francis Brown, S. R. Driver, Charles A. Briggs, James Strong, and Wilhelm Gesenius, *The Brown-Driver-Briggs Hebrew and English Lexicon: With an Appendix Containing the Biblical Aramaic: Coded with the Numbering System from Strong's Exhaustive Concordance of the Bible* (Hendrickson, 1996), 1072–73.

65. Richard M. Davidson, *Flame of Yahweh: Sexuality in the Old Testament* (Hendrickson, 2007), 171.

66. Davidson, *Flame of Yahweh*, 171. See also the arguments of Peter J. Harland, "Menswear and Womenswear: A Study of Deuteronomy 22:5," *ExpTim* 110 (1998): 74–75.

67. Carl Friedrich Keil and Franz Delitzsch, *Commentary on the Old Testament* (Hendrickson, 2002), 1.945.

68. Harland, "Menswear and Womenswear," 76.

69. *Transsexuality: A Report by the Evangelical Alliance Policy Commission* (Evangelical Alliance, 2000), 47. In fairness to the report, it then goes on to modify its own verdict and in a helpful footnote admits that "we need to be careful not to dilute Scripture at this point."

70. Daniel I. Block, *The NIV Application Commentary: Deuteronomy* (Zondervan, 2012), 512. The issues of intention and effect also require consid-

eration. That is, might it be possible to engage in cross-dressing for (say) the purpose of entertainment without the intention or effect of confusing either self or others or "blurring established boundaries"? Perhaps. But there are obvious risks. While intentions can be innocuous, effects are much harder to predict and impossible to control.

71. See Gordon J. Wenham, "The Old Testament Attitude to Homosexuality," *ExpTim* 102 (1990–91): 359–63.

72. Roy E. Ciampa and Brian S. Rosner, *The First Letter to the Corinthians* (Eerdmans, 2010), 241. Hence the LEB's rendering: "nor passive homosexual partners, nor dominant homosexual partners."

73. Robert J. Gagnon, *The Bible and Homosexual Practice* (Abingdon, 2002), 311. This is why translating *malakoi* as "male prostitutes" (as does the ASV and ISV) is unjustifiably narrow.

74. William Loader, *The New Testament on Sexuality* (Eerdmans, 2012), 328–29.

75. Gagnon, *The Bible and Homosexual Practice*, 312.

76. For example, commentators debate whether Paul is talking about head coverings, veils, or hairstyles, whether his teaching applies only to husbands and wives or to men and women more broadly, and what he means by "because of the angels" in v. 10. For a clear, scholarly and accessible exposition of both the meaning and implications of this chap-

ter, see Claire Smith, *God's Good Design: What the Bible Says About Men and Women* (Matthias Media, 2012), 53–80.

77. Ciampa and Rosner, *The First Letter to the Corinthians*, 503.

78. This, according to Anthony Thiselton, is why Paul "expresses no less disquiet (probably indeed more) about men whose style is effeminate with possible hints of a quasihomosexual blurring of male gender than about women who likewise reject the use of signals of respectable and respected gender distinctiveness." Anthony C. Thiselton, *The First Epistle to the Corinthians*, NIGTC (Eerdmans, 2000), 805.

79. T. R. Schreiner, "Head Coverings, Prophecies and the Trinity," in *Recovering Biblical Manhood and Womanhood: A Response to Evangelical Feminism,* ed. John Piper and Wayne Grudem (Crossway, 1991), 138–39.

80. Smith, *God's Good Design*, 78.

81. Schreiner, "Head Coverings, Prophecies and the Trinity," 138.

82. Richard Bauckham, *God and the Crisis of Freedom: Biblical and Contemporary Perspectives* (John Knox, 2002), 70.

83. As Oliver O'Donovan writes: "New creation is creation renewed, a restoration and enhancement, not an abolition" ("Creation, Redemption and Nature—

Web Sermon 6," *Fulcrum: Renew the Evangelical Centre* (December 9, 2006), https://www.fulcrum -anglican.org.uk/articles/creation-redemption-and -nature-web-sermon-6.

84. I say "largely" because it is impossible to disentangle the "complex interplay of nature, nurture, environment, and choices. Incremental choices made in response to impulses may strengthen the same impulses." See R. J. Gagnon, "How Should Christians Respond to the Transgender Phenomenon," *First Things* (October 16, 2015), https://www .firstthings.com/web-exclusives/2015/10/how -should-christians-respond-to-the-transgender -phenomenon.

85. Not surprisingly, the instance of "sex-change regret" is disturbingly high (and little publicized) and, tragically, the experience of undergoing "gender transition" seems to do little to address the high attempted-suicide rate of transgender people (over 40 percent). In fact, one longitudinal Swedish study (published in 2011) found the attempted-suicide rate following transition was some twenty times that of comparable peers. See Cecilia Dhejne, Paul Lichtenstein, Marcus Boman, Anna L. V. Johansson, Niklas Långström, and Mikael Landén, "Long-Term Follow-Up of Transsexual Persons Undergoing Sex Reassignment Surgery: Cohort Study in Sweden," *PLoS One* 6.2 (February 22,

2011), http://www.ncbi.nlm.nih.gov/pmc/articles/PMC3043071.

86. John Calvin, *Institutes of the Christian Religion* 1, ed. J. T. McNeill; trans. F. L. Battles; 2 vols. (Westminster, 1960), vol. 1, 737 (3.11.10).

87. Contra Mark A. Yarhouse, "Understanding the Transgender Phenomenon," *Christianity Today* (June 8, 2015), http://www.christianitytoday.com/ct/2015/july-august/understanding-transgender-gender-dysphoria.html. In response to Yarhouse, Robert Gagnon puts the point strongly but helpfully: "while redemption is unmerited, an active pursuit of a 'transgender' life would be at odds with minimal standards for repentance, faith, transformation, and a claim to 'faithfulness' to Christ." Robert A. J. Gagnon, "Gender Dysphoria and 'Practical Application': A Rejoinder to Mark Yarhouse" (August 28, 2016), http://www.robgagnon.net/Yarhouse%20Rejoinder.htm.

88. See further J. Todd Billings, *Rejoicing in Lament: Wrestling with Incurable Cancer and Life in Christ* (Brazos, 2015); Kelly M. Kapic, *Embodied Hope: A Theological Meditation on Pain and Suffering* (IVP Academic, 2017); Robert S. Smith, "Belting Out the Blues as Believers: The Importance of Singing Lament," *Themelios* 42.1 (2017): 89–111.

89. Oliver O'Donovan, "Transsexualism and Christian Marriage," *Journal of Religious Ethics* 11.1 (1983): 151.

90. John Wyatt, *Matters of Life and Death: Human Dilemmas in the light of the Christian faith* (IVP, 2009), 98.

91. Wyatt, *Matters of Life and Death,* 100. Furthermore, as O'Donovan argues ("Transsexualism and Christian Marriage," 152), "Whatever the surgeon may be able to do, and whatever he may yet learn to do, he cannot make self out of not-self. He cannot turn an artifact into a human being's body. The transsexual can never say with justice: 'These organs are my bodily being, and their sex is my sex.'"

92. Richard P. Fitzgibbons, Philip M. Sutton, and Dale O'Leary, "The Psychopathology of 'Sex Reassignment' Surgery: Assessing Its Medical, Psychological, and Ethical Appropriateness," *The National Catholic Bioethics Quarterly* 9.1 (2009): 97.

93. Fitzgibbons, Sutton, and O'Leary, "The Psychopathology of 'Sex Reassignment' Surgery," 98.

94. R. Bränström and J. E. Pachankis, "Reduction in Mental Health Treatment Utilization Among Transgender Individuals After Gender-Affirming Surgeries: A Total Population Study," *Am J Psychiatry* (August 1, 2020), 177(8): 727–34.

95. Given the alarmingly high rate of post-transition suicide attempts and the prevalence of psychiatric disorders in persons who successfully suicide, the claim that withholding hormonal or surgical treat-

ment increases suicide risk is misleading. Preston Sprinkle is therefore right to conclude: "In the conversation about trans* suicidality, ignoring the prevalence of co-occurring mental health concerns and laying emphasis exclusively on transitioning may seem caring and respectful, but it does no favors to the trans* community" (Sprinkle, *Embodied*, 235–36). See also J. M. Bertolote and A. Fleischmann, "Suicide and psychiatric diagnosis: a worldwide perspective," *World Psychiatry* (2002), 1(3): 181–85; Mayer and McHugh, "Sexuality and Gender," 106–13.

96. Mark A. Yarhouse, *Understanding Gender Dysphoria: Navigating Transgender Issues in a Changing Culture* (IVP, 2015), 151.

97. Yarhouse, "Understanding the Transgender Phenomenon."

98. See further, Robert S. Smith, "Discipleship and the Transgender Convert: Issues and Proposals," *Eikon* (Fall 2019): 60–74, https://cbmw.org/2019/11/20/discipleship-and-the-transgengender-convert-issues-and-proposals; Sprinkle, *Embodied*, 81–96.

99. See Richard Hove, "Does Galatians 3:28 Negate Gender-Specific Roles?," 105–43; and Daniel R. Heimbach, "The Unchangeable Difference: Eternally Fixed Sexual Identity for an Age of Plastic Sexuality," 275–89. Both essays are found in Wayne

Grudem, ed., *Biblical Foundations for Manhood and Womanhood* (Crossway, 2002).

100. Indeed, Jesus' confirmation of the fact that Abraham, Isaac, and Jacob remain Abraham, Isaac, and Jacob beyond the grave (v. 32; compare Exod 3:6) points to the continuity of their sex-determined gender identity in the age to come.

101. Augustine, *The City of God*, 19.22.17.

102. Mark David Walton, "What We Shall Be: A Look at Gender and the New Creation," *JBMW* 9/1 (Spring 2004), 19.

103. As to the idea that the intersexed will be raised as intersexed, this would seem to fly in the face of the fact that all diseases, disorders, and disabilities will be healed in the resurrection.

104. Matthew Mason, "The Wounded It Heals: Gender Dysphoria and the Resurrection of the Body," in *Beauty, Order, and Mystery: A Christian Vision of Human Sexuality*, ed. Gerald Hiestand and Todd Wilson (IVP, 2017), 143. Emphasis original.

105. Karl Barth, *Church Dogmatics*, 4 vols in 14 part-volumes, ed. Geoffrey W. Bromiley and Thomas F. Torrance; trans. Geoffrey W. Bromiley. (T&T Clark, 1975), III/I, 195.

106. C. C. Roberts, *Creation and Covenant: The Significance of Sexual Difference in the Moral Theology of Marriage* (T&T Clark, 2007), 165–66.

107. This is *why* it appears, and *how* it is classified, in the most recent edition of the *Diagnostic and Statistical Manual of Mental Disorders*. However, the weakness of *DSM*-V, as we've already noted, is that it is only the dysphoria or distress that is seen as the clinical problem, not the gender incongruence itself (as was the case in *DSM*-IV). This leads to a focus on alleviating the consequence (distress) rather than attempt to resolve the condition (incongruence) causing the distress. However, there are stronger reasons for regarding gender incongruence itself (irrespective of the distress it may or may not cause) as a mental disorder. This was the helpfulness of the category of *Gender Identity Disorder* in *DSM*-IV.

108. See further, Sprinkle, *Embodied*, 129–54.

109. Paul McHugh, "Transgenderism: A Pathogenic Meme," *Public Discourse* (June 10, 2015), http://www.thepublicdiscourse.com/2015/06/15145.

110. McHugh, "Transgenderism."

111. Russell Moore, "Joan or John? My Answer: Part Two," *Russell Moore* (May 26, 2009), http://www.russellmoore.com/2009/05/26/joan-or-john-my-answer-part-two.

112. Nick Cater, "Queer Teen Craze," *Spectator Australia* (January 30, 2021), https://www.spectator.com.au/2021/01/queer-teen-craze. Cater uses the word "insanity" rather than "folly."

113. R. Albert Mohler Jr., *We Cannot Be Silent: Speaking Truth to a Culture Redefining Sex, Marriage, and the Very Meaning of Right and Wrong* (Nelson Books, 2015).

LEXHAM PRESS

CLARIFYING ANSWERS ON QUESTIONS FOR RESTLESS MINDS

Series Editor: D. A. Carson

The Questions for Restless Minds series applies God's word to today's issues. Each short book faces tough questions honestly and clearly, so you can think wisely, act with conviction, and become more like Christ.

Learn more at lexhampress.com/questions